Library of
Davidson College

D1523904

INTERNATIONAL BANK FOR RECONSTRUCTION AND DEVELOPMENT

WORLD BANK STAFF OCCASIONAL PAPERS NUMBER EIGHT

JACK BARANSON

# AUTOMOTIVE INDUSTRIES IN DEVELOPING COUNTRIES

*Distributed by The Johns Hopkins Press*
*Baltimore, Maryland*

338.4
B225a

Copyright © 1969
by the International Bank for Reconstruction and Development
All rights reserved
Manufactured in the United States of America
Library of Congress Catalog Card Number 77–85339
Standard Book Number 8018-1086-8

70-3478

# FOREWORD

I would like to explain *why* the World Bank Group does research work, and why it publishes it. We feel an obligation to look beyond the projects we help to finance towards the whole resource allocation of an economy, and the effectiveness of the use of those resources. Our major concern, in dealings with member countries, is that all scarce resources, including capital, skilled labor, enterprise and know-how, should be used to their best advantage. We want to see policies that encourage appropriate increases in the supply of savings, whether domestic or international. Finally, we are required by our Articles, as well as by inclination, to use objective economic criteria in all our judgments.

These are our preoccupations, and these, one way or another, are the subjects of most of our research work. Clearly, they are also the proper concern of anyone who is interested in promoting development, and so we seek to make our research papers widely available. In doing so, we have to take the risk of being misunderstood. Although these studies are published by the Bank, the views expressed and the methods explored should not necessarily be considered to represent the Bank's views or policies. Rather they are offered as a modest contribution to the great discussion on how to advance the economic development of the underdeveloped world.

ROBERT S. McNAMARA
President
International Bank for Reconstruction and Development

v

# TABLE OF CONTENTS

TABLES

CHARTS

ANNEX TABLES

# PREFACE

The study on the automotive industries is one of three case studies prepared as part of a broader research project dealing with the experience of developing countries with the establishment of capital goods industries, which was under the direction of Barend A. de Vries. The case studies dealing with automotive, heavy electrical and mechanical equipment industries were directed by Bertil Walstedt. Herman van der Tak reviewed the studies in their later phase.

The industries selected for case studies play a strategic role in the more advanced phases of industrial development. Their establishment takes up a substantial share of investment and is, therefore, often accompanied by strains on real and financial resources and poses difficult problems of domestic and external economic policies. In addition, these industries produce many items used in the construction of the kind of projects financed by the Bank.

The industry studies were designed to consider the following questions:

—What has been the experience thus far of the industry in countries with relatively small markets?

—What are the economics of the industry in more advanced industrial countries and what are the conditions of international markets for the products concerned? What aspects are relevant for the growth of the industries in the developing countries?

—What are the costs and benefits of establishing these industries in developing countries? In particular, what is the cost of the saving of foreign exchange made possible by the industry?

—What can be said about the efficiency of the industry, at present and over time, and how is cost efficiency affected by such industrial factors as economies of scale, availability of supplier capabilities, skilled manpower, product design, access to new technology?

—What has been the impact upon the industry's cost efficiency of government policies—protection, exchange and import regulation, requirements as to domestic content of production, credit, etc.—as well as of the structure and the extent of monopoly of domestic industry?

—What general indications, if any, can be given on policies of developing countries, as well as of industrialized countries to foster the healthy growth of the industry?

—What contributions might reasonably be expected from large multinational firms in promoting manufacturing in developing countries?

—What is the future outlook for the industries in an international context and what might be the manufacturing role of developing countries?

Because of the nature of the problems to be analyzed, heavy reliance had to be placed on direct interviews with, and information provided by, manufacturing concerns in developing countries and associated or parent firms in advanced industrial countries. In the case of the automotive industry visits to developing countries were limited to Argentina and Yugoslavia, but interviews with multinational companies covered their operations in much of the developing world.

We are grateful to the various company representatives for their generous and invaluable assistance. They have shown great interest in the studies, have discussed the problems of the industry with frankness and made available information without which the study could not have been undertaken. They have supplied comments and criticisms on an earlier draft, permitting us to test the validity of the analysis and the accuracy of the factual information used.

The present study was carried out by Mr. Jack Baranson. His findings and recommendations are based on field work in Argentina, Yugoslavia and New Zealand, supplemented by interviews with vehicle and parts manufacturers in Europe and North America and documentation available in the Bank. The author was also able to draw on his research work carried out prior to joining the Bank and published as *Manufacturing Problems in India* (Syracuse University Press, 1967) and *Technology for Developing Economies* (Pergamon Press, 1967). Mr. Sani El Darwish (of the International Finance Corporation) accompanied the author on his visits to several firms in Europe and generously contributed his thorough knowledge and experience of the industry. Mr. Hector Turay assisted in preparing the tables and charts that appear in the study. There were also helpful criticisms and suggestions by automotive vehicle manufacturers and by other experts both inside and outside the World Bank Group. However, the author alone is responsible for the facts and opinions presented, which should not be taken as necessarily representing the views of the Bank.

ANDREW M. KAMARCK
Director
Economics Department

# I

# INTRODUCTION

1.  This study is concerned with the relative cost and efficiency of manufacturing various types of transport equipment under the conditions that prevail in newly industrializing economies. An effort has been made to obtain a broad view of commercial strategies and operational models which could be applied to such countries. The study also provides a framework which could be used for economic analysis of industrial projects in other economic sectors.[1]

2.  Field work was carried out in some developing countries and among the major manufacturers in Europe and North America. The author spent a month in Argentina in late 1965 and visited Yugoslavia briefly in late 1966. Cost data were obtained from India through correspondence with vehicle manufacturers there. In Argentina, both government and corporate officials were interviewed to get a balanced view of the impact of industrialization policies upon manufacturing operations. Each of the major firms in Argentina prepared a written response to an outline questionnaire. These written reports were supplemented by a series of interviews with the plant managers. A similar procedure was followed in Yugoslavia. Interviews with international firms were based upon an outline questionnaire which was distributed beforehand.

---

[1] See the sector analysis on steel, automotive, and pulp and paper industries in Chapter 5, *The World Bank Report on the New Zealand Economy 1968,* Government Printer (Wellington, N.Z.).

1

More than 50 vehicle and parts manufacturers were visited in late 1966. Talks were held mainly with corporate executives concerned both with the financial and with the technical aspects of overseas manufacturing operations in developing countries. Finally, the author visited New Zealand in 1968 as a member of the World Bank mission.

3. The problem of the relative cost and efficiency of manufacturing industries in developing areas has received growing attention in recent years. Several studies are now underway or nearing completion, especially those headed by I. M. D. Little at the O.E.C.D. and Nuffield College on industrialization, by Joseph Grunwald and Martin Carney at the Brookings Institution on comparative production costs, and by Bela Balassa at the World Bank on the structure of effective tariff levels in several countries. Important work in the field has also been done by David Felix of Washington University and Stephen Lewis's group at Williams College on the effects of import substitution. Two published studies on the automotive industry (both doctoral theses from the Harvard Graduate School of Business Administration) also have special relevance to this study. One is by Guillermo S. Edelberg, *The Procurement Practices of the Mexican Affiliates of Selected United States Automobile Firm* (June 1963); and the other is by Sebastiaan J. Kleu, *Import Substitution in the South African Automobile Industry* (June 1967). Many of the issues covered in this study were considered at a *Seminar on the Establishment and Development of the Automotive Industry in Developing Countries*, sponsored by the United Nations Industrial Development Organization in Karlovy Vary, Czechoslovakia, 24 February–7 March 1969. See also the comprehensive study by the Argentine Economic Study Commission on the Automotive Industry, *Factors that Distort the Establishment of Costs in the Argentine Automotive Industry* (draft manuscript, Buenos Aires, December 1968).

## FOCUS OF STUDY

4. Specifically, this study concentrates on the following aspects of automotive sector development: (a) the comparative costs of production, (b) the adaptation problems of manufacturing affiliates, and (c) the impact of economic policy upon market structure. It became evident in the early stages of investigation that the role of international corporations had been vital in the historical development of the automotive industries and were essential to future change. This was particularly true for national economies that had exhausted growth opportunities based upon import substitution in domestic markets and were now anxious to reduce resource costs and possibly expand output for world markets. It is for this reason that the marketing and manufacturing strategies

2

of international corporations and their adjustment problems in developing economies have been examined in depth.

5.   One of the conclusions that emerges from the study is that sound economic and commercial policy is as important to industrial progress as is success in overcoming critical shortages or deficiencies in financial resources, production factors, managerial and engineering skills, and supplier capabilities. A corollary to this conclusion is that the pattern generally followed by developing economies in establishing their automotive industries needs critical scrutiny.

6.   For countries that have already established an automotive industry, possible new patterns of manufacturing and trade are suggested. For countries about to establish an automotive industry, the increased costs of import substitution in terms of internal resources and foreign exchange are indicated. The analysis probes beyond the conventional framework of cost and feasibility at the plant level, to try to assess the impact of market structure upon the efficiency of resource utilization. The cost analysis and recommendations for reorganizing the automotive industry should have application to other industrial sectors too.

## PROBLEMS AND LIMITATIONS

7.   Most of the empirical evidence presented in this study should not be taken as conclusive proof of a general principle. To begin with, there is a very wide range of conditions and circumstances among plants, product mixes, and national environments, compared to the narrow base that could be surveyed with the time and resources available. Field work in developing countries was limited to Argentina and Yugoslavia. The substantial experience of Japanese firms in developing countries has not been covered. Secondly, the automotive industry covers a great variety of vehicles ranging from small passenger cars to heavy commercial trucks. There are often considerable differences in engineering sophistication and in volume requirements which affect the economies of production by world standards. Automotive vehicle production is also often integrated with the manufacture of railroad and tractor equipment or lighter vehicles such as motorcycles—products generally excluded from this study, although incidental reference is made to them where relevant. Thirdly, the intricacies of cost analysis limit the conclusiveness of evidence.

8.   Obtaining a satisfactory set of comprehensive cost data was a major problem. Fortunately a very fine set of data was finally obtained from an American manufacturer which compared actual production costs in Argentina, Brazil,

3

and Mexico to costs for a comparable vehicle manufactured and assembled in the United States. Costs were broken down for each of the four countries: (a) by cost inputs, i.e. labor, material, and other categories, (b) by successive stages of domestic content (from assembly through body stamping), and (c) by actual resource cost and transfer costs (taxes and tariffs). But only one set of such data was obtained.

9. Several other complexities are described in the chapter on cost comparisons. Among the more prominent are the distorting effect upon cost comparisons of an overvalued exchange rate and of indirect tariff and tax charges that are often difficult to trace and attribute accurately. (The calculation of additional resource costs to arrive at domestic value added is necessary to determine actual or projected protection required.) Nor has it always been possible to distinguish among cost increases induced by disproportionately high protectionist profits, learning curve effects, technical inefficiencies caused by differences in scale or productivity, and the distorting effects of price structure referred to above. Definitive appraisal of levels of efficiency, current and prospective, would require more precise weighting of each of these elements.

10. The economic, commercial, and technical factors involved in vehicle production and national resource utilization are entangled. Thus at least three sets of decision makers are involved in policies which affect the cost and efficiency of production. These include: governmental authorities issuing industrial licenses, controlling imports, and in other ways affecting price and market structure; international firms concerned with maximizing international profits; and manufacturing affiliates in the developing economy whose profits are realized in a protected and controlled economy.

11. It is not easy to isolate the effects of different national policies and measures which constrict the economics of manufacturing. The evidence in Argentina and Yugoslavia in particular indicates that the economics of manufacturing is meshed with broader national policies for investment in transport and with tax policy intended to influence the private consumption of automotive products. In Japan, it is evident that the industry was moulded by national policies designed to discourage the consumption and production of private passenger cars, to favor instead the manufacture of commercial trucks, and thereby also to defer investments in road in favor of rail transport systems.[2]

---

[2] See Katsuji Kawamata, "The Automobile Industry and Current Problems," *Keidanren Review*, Vol. 2, No. 7 (Japan, 1967), pp. 29–37; and "Japan: Special Survey: 2," *The Economist* (June 9, 1967), pp. xxi-xxii. See also para. 148.

12.   The analysis in this study develops what economists would call a "second-best" solution. The study starts with the question, given a determination to develop an automotive industry, how may sector efficiency be maximized at successive levels of resource commitment? Stated another way, manufacturing and marketing strategies are sought which should permit the *industry* to operate in the range of maximum comparative advantage. The study does not deal with the question of total costs of automobile consumption, which may include investments in roads and fuel imports, nor with the even broader issue of social investment in alternative means of transport. Nor does it deal with the question of the alternative use of economic resources in other sectors or activities. For example, in the chapter on Argentina, the question is not whether the economy should concentrate on beef production and eliminate the automotive industry entirely. It is rather what are the limits of import substitution in Argentina's automotive sector, and how can production be restructured or rationalized so as to reduce resource costs for a given volume or international value of output in automotive products?

## OUTLINE OF CHAPTERS

13.   Chapter II analyzes the quantitative aspects of supply and demand in automotive products by developing economies viewed in the world context. Chapter III analyzes recent changes in the market structure of developing economies and the problems incurred by international firms in adapting to the described changes. Chapter IV analyzes the relevant characteristics of automotive products and production techniques and the problems posed in establishing manufacturing affiliates in newly industrializing or small-scale economies. The heart of the analysis is contained in Chapter V on comparative costs. It demonstrates that inefficiency in automotive production is largely due to the inefficiency of small-scale production of components and parts, and that average total costs increase proportionally to the diseconomies of scale imposed by the domestic content requirement.

14.   Chapters VI, VII, and VIII are country studies on Argentina, Yugoslavia, and New Zealand. Argentina provides a classic case of the adverse effects of import substitution policies pursued to a degree which results in progressive increases in resource costs and an unmanageable foreign exchange burden. Yugoslavia is interesting as a newly industrializing economy that has itself become a transmitter of industrial technology in the automotive field and is now experimenting with programs to reorganize and nationalize industry

5

along more efficient lines. New Zealand helps to demonstrate the effect of protection upon a small-scale economy that is otherwise "developed."

15. The last chapter contains conclusions and recommendations. It begins with a critique of the effects of protection, moves on to an evaluation of possible changes in market structure to improve the economic efficiency of automotive production, and ends with suggestions for further research.

# II

## WORLD DEMAND AND SUPPLY OF
## CARS AND TRUCKS

16.   Automotive products consist of a wide array of passenger cars, trucks, and buses. Trucks range from light-weight pickups to multi-ton trailers, and buses from small minibuses to large double-deckers used for urban and inter-urban transport. Motorcycles, three-wheeled vehicles and farm tractors are not included in this study, even though they are often manufactured or marketed together with other automotive products, especially in developing countries. For example, in Argentina, Fiat manufactures passenger cars, diesel engines, farm tractors, and railroad equipment in a single industrial complex; in Sahagun, Mexico, passenger cars, buses, trucks, diesel engines, and railroad equipment are also manufactured in a single industrial complex. In analyzing demand, a distinction needs to be drawn between vehicles purchased for commercial use and for private consumption. On the production side, there are considerable differences in the production scales and unit costs of the high-volume production of passenger cars and light trucks and the much lower-volume production of medium to heavy trucks, buses and other commercial vehicles. Differences in volume requirements and engineering sophistication have a bearing upon the potential comparative advantage range for developing or small-scale economies.

17.   In 1965, developing countries accounted for only a small fraction of world production (about 4 percent) and consumption (about 6 percent) of

7

automotive vehicles. The United States accounted for 44 percent of world production and 46 percent of world consumption of passenger cars and trucks. Five other countries (Germany, the United Kingdom, Japan, France, and Italy) manufactured another 39 percent and consumed 27 percent of the world totals. This left about 17 percent produced and 27 percent consumed in all other countries of the world. About half of the 25 million vehicles manufactured in 1965 went to replace old cars, and half to meet increased demand. It appears that most of the replacement purchases were in the developed countries; purchases in the developing countries were to meet growing demand:

|  | Produced, 1965 | Consumed, 1965 |
|---|---|---|
| United States | 11.1 million (44.3%) | 11.5 (46.2%) |
| Germany, United Kingdom, Japan, France, Italy | 9.8 (39.1%) | 7.0 (27.2%) |
| Developing countries | 1.0 (4.0%) | 1.5[a] (5.9%) |
| All other countries | 3.3 (12.6%) | 5.1 (20.7%) |
| Total | 25.1 | 25.1 |

[a] Author's estimate.

*Source:* McGraw-Hill, *1966 World Automotive Industry*, and A.M.A., *World Motor Vehicle Data 1966*. At the date of going to press in April 1969, neither authority had yet published complete figures for 1967, let alone 1968. We have used 1965 figures because they are a comprehensive and compatible set, and because the study was based on the world position in that year. 1965 was a peak year in world production.

## WORLD DEMAND

18. There were over 170 million cars and trucks registered in non-Communist countries as of January 1, 1966. About 12 percent were in the developing countries and the remaining 88 percent in the industrialized countries. Vehicle population in developing countries has been growing at nearly double the rate of that in industrialized economies during the past 15 years:

|  | Vehicle Registration | | Percent Distribution | Average Annual Rate of Growth, % |
|---|---|---|---|---|
|  | 1950 | 1966 | 1966 | 1950–66 |
| Industrialized countries (USA, Canada, Western Europe, and Oceania) | 56.1 | 152.3 | 88 | 6.2 |
| Industrializing countries (Africa, Asia,[a] and Latin America) | 3.5 | 21.0 | 12 | 11.7 |
| Total | 59.6 | 173.3 | 100 | 6.9 |

[a] Includes Japan; 6.8 million in 1966, or 4 percent of the total.
*Source:* Annex Table 2.

8

19. Developing economies, relatively low in per capita income, have been rapidly increasing their per capita consumption of vehicles. In 1965, Argentina and Spain, among the developing economies, ranked high in vehicle density:

| Country | Inhabitants per Vehicle |
|---|---|
| United States | 2 |
| New Zealand | 3 |
| Germany | 6 |
| Argentina | 14 |
| Japan | 15 |
| Spain | 27 |
| Mexico | 38 |
| Brazil | 41 |
| Yugoslavia | 77 |
| India | 479 |

*Source:* Annex Table 3.

The prices of the most popular cars are much more in line with the purchasing power of factory workers in Mexico than they are in Argentina or Brazil:

| Country | Most Popular Vehicle | Percent of Auto Worker's Annual Income Required |
|---|---|---|
| Italy | Fiat 500 | 30 |
| Germany | Volkswagen | 43 |
| Mexico | Volkswagen (Mexican) | 63 |
| Japan | Toyota Corona | 72 |
| Brazil | Volkswagen (Brazilian) | 138 |
| Argentina | Fiat 1500 (Argentine) | 233 |

*Source:* Annex Table 22.

## WORLD PRODUCTION

20. World production of cars, trucks, and buses totaled 25.2 million in 1965—about 20.0 million passenger cars and 5.2 million trucks and buses (Annex Table 1). For the major commercial vehicle producers of the world, about 25 percent of output is in the six-ton-and-over class or medium-to-heavy class.[1] Developing countries produced a larger share of trucks and buses than of passenger car vehicles:

---

[1]Automobile Manufacturers Association, *World Motor Vehicle Data* (1965); "Commercial Vehicles, a Special Survey," *The Economist* (July 14, 1967); Dana Corporation, *Automotive News, 1966 Almanac.*

*Production in 1965 (million units)*

|  | Passenger Cars | Trucks, Buses | Total |
|---|---|---|---|
| Developed countries | 18.9 | 4.3 | 23.1 |
|  | (95.0%) | (82.7%) | (92.0%) |
| Communist countries | 0.4 | 0.5 | 1.0 |
|  | (2.0%) | (9.6%) | (4.0%) |
| Developing countries | 0.6 | 0.4 | 1.0 |
|  | (3.0%) | (7.7%) | (4.0%) |
| All countries | 19.9 | 5.2 | 25.1 |
|  | (100.0%) | (100.0%) | (100.0%) |

*Source:* Annex Table 1.

21.    Automotive production in industrialized economies is mainly in the hands of large firms. This is especially true of high-volume production of cars and trucks. Two American firms accounted for over a third of world production, 9 other firms for an additional third, and the remaining third was manufactured by over 300 companies located in 50 or more countries:

| Number of Firms, 1965 | Volume Range per Firm p.a., (Units) | Average Volume per Firm p.a. |
|---|---|---|
| 2 | 3,100,000–5,700,000 | 4,400,000 |
| 9 | 500,000–1,600,000 | 856,000 |
| 14 | 200,000–   400,000 | 257,000 |
| 293 | below    200,000 | 14,000 |
| 318 | – | 76,000 |

*Source:* Annex Table 5.

22.    Production volumes range between 100,000 and 1,500,000 per annum among the 23 medium-size passenger car manufacturers, and between 13,000 and 150,000 among the 42 medium-size truck and bus manufacturers. Four firms in developing countries appeared in the rank listing of the 44 leading truck manufacturers of the world: Willys of Brazil (32),[2] Citroën of Spain (35), Industrias Kaiser of Argentina (37),[2] and Tata Mercedes of India (30).

23.    In 1966, the 7 major producing countries had 387 vehicle assembly lines in 55 countries (Annex Table 6), as compared to only 170 assembly lines in 42 countries six years earlier. The Japanese (especially Toyota and Nissan)

---

[2] Willys of Brazil is now an affiliate of Ford and Industrias Kaiser Argentina of Renault.

have been especially aggressive in this field; they increased overseas assembly lines from 7 in 6 countries in 1962 to 49 lines in 22 countries in 1966. European producers (Sweden, West Germany, France, United Kingdom, and Italy) exported one-half to one-third of their output, in contrast to the United States which exported less than 2 percent and Japan which averaged just over 10 percent in 1965:

| | *All Vehicles* | | *Exports as Percent of Production* |
|---|---|---|---|
| *Country* | *Production* | *Exports* | |
| Sweden | 204,000 | 108,100 | 53.0 |
| West Germany | 3,055,700 | 1,527,300 | 50.0 |
| France | 1,581,600 | 613,000 | 38.8 |
| United Kingdom | 2,134,900 | 793,800 | 37.2 |
| Italy | 1,158,200 | 326,700 | 28.8 |
| Canada | 849,000 | 96,200 | 11.3 |
| Japan | 1,870,500 | 194,200 | 10.4 |
| Australia | 352,900 | 12,383 | 3.5 |
| USA | 11,112,000 | 167,700 | 1.5 |

*Sources:* McGraw-Hill, *World Automotive Market Survey, 1966*, Automobile Manufacturers Association, Inc., *World Motor Vehicle Data*, 1965.

## PRODUCTION IN DEVELOPING COUNTRIES

24.  Among the developing countries, the five leading producers in 1965 were Spain, Argentina, Brazil, Mexico and India. Together they accounted for 80 percent of the near one million vehicles manufactured and assembled in varying degrees by developing economies. Another 83,500 vehicles were assembled and partially manufactured in 18 other developing countries, with some countries turning out as few as 1,000 vehicles a year. At least 200 firms in over 25 countries were engaged in vehicle production (Annex Table 1). Spain, Argentina, and Brazil have been increasing domestic product at particularly high annual rates of growth:

| | *Vehicles Manufactured, 1965* | *Annual Production Growth Rate, 1955–65* |
|---|---|---|
| | | *(percent)* |
| Japan | 1,876,000 | 39 |
| Argentina | 195,000 | 35 |
| Spain | 229,000 | 29 |
| Brazil | 186,000 | 25 |
| Germany | 3,056,000 | 13 |
| New Zealand | 72,000 | 13 |
| Mexico | 97,000 | 12 |
| India | 70,000 | 9 |
| United States | 11,138,000 | 2 |

*Source:* Annex Table 7.

11

25. Average production volumes of firms accounting for the large part of output in developing economies are quite low by European and Japanese standards, to say nothing of US volumes. These averages have special relevance for economies of scale in the manufacture of passenger cars and light trucks. Averages cited in the table below include a small percentage of the heavier vehicles, where economies of scale begin at a much lower threshold:

TABLE 1: Vehicle Production Volumes, European and Developing Countries, 1965

|  | Number of Firms Accounting for 80–90% of National Production in 1965 | Average Units per Firm |
|---|---|---|
| Italy | 1 | 988,000 |
| West Germany | 4 | 649,000 |
| United Kingdom | 4 | 498,000 |
| France | 4 | 383,000 |
| Japan | 8 | 211,000 |
| Spain | 3 | 60,000 |
| Brazil | 3 | 54,000 |
| Argentina | 6 | 28,000 |
| Mexico | 6 | 19,000 |
| India | 5 | 11,000 |
| Venezuela | 6 | 8,000 |
| New Zealand | 7 | 8,000 |

Source: McGraw-Hill, *1966 World Automotive Market Survey.*

# III

## ADAPTATION PROBLEMS OF
## INTERNATIONAL CORPORATIONS

26.  Since 1950, there has been a significant trend toward the manufacture and assembly of automotive products by the developing countries to satisfy their own needs, largely because of a desire to reduce imports. The spread of production facilities throughout the world is dramatic. One major European vehicle manufacturer has reported that about 94 percent of its export earnings came from about 20 countries (mostly industrialized); the remaining 6 percent was earned in over 100 countries (mostly developing areas). For most international firms, corporate earnings from developing countries account for only a small percentage of total earnings. But a manufacturing affiliate in a developing country represents a sizable customer for components and parts even for a large international firm.[1]

---

[1] The value of sales of US overseas manufacturing subsidiaries was estimated at $150 billion in 1966. Of this amount as much as $15 billion or more—out of $30 billion total US exports in 1967—may represent the sales value of components, parts, and manufacturing equipment sold to overseas industrial affiliates (based upon an estimate that 11 percent of sales by Latin American affiliates represent imports from the United States). See Judd Polk, *US Exports and US Production Abroad*, staff memo prepared for the United States Council of the International Chamber of Commerce (August 11, 1967).

13

# CHANGES IN SUPPLY STRUCTURE
## FOR MARKETS IN DEVELOPING COUNTRIES

27.   International firms have gone through two phases in their market relations with developing countries, and are now entering a third phase in the more advanced areas. Where market conditions warranted, assembly operations were undertaken in selected countries by major manufacturers following World War I. General Motors built assembly plants in Argentina, Brazil and India during the 1920's and in Egypt, Mexico and Spain during the 1930's. But prior to World War II, international firms for the most part manufactured automotive products in their home country and exported them to overseas markets. In the second phase, which began in the mid 50's, automotive manufacturers were forced by developing countries either to expand local manufacturing or lose the domestic market. In the past year or two, foreign firms have found themselves being urged into "Phase III." Certain developing countries, such as Mexico and Yugoslavia, have been bargaining for export capacities to be built into their manufacturing operations to help pay for continuing import requirements. In this they have in effect followed the lead of Canada whose trade agreement with the United States has resulted in a substantial increase in Canadian parts manufacture for the US market (para. 134).

28.   The requirement to develop overseas manufacturing capacities has posed some basic dilemmas for international firms. One dilemma stems from the duplication of small-scale production facilities throughout the world at a time when competitive conditions and technology are moving firms toward corporate mergers and concentration of production facilities. Among industrialized economies, rising wages and technological progress have forced corporate mergers and the adoption of high-volume production techniques in most parts of the world. Yet at the same period of time, developing countries have insisted upon the creation of national automotive industries requiring small-scale assembly and parts plants using labor-intensive techniques. A second dilemma relates to the need to redesign products and techniques to meet specialized demands in small-scale markets. But the size of markets is often too small to warrant the additional expenditures to adapt product designs or production techniques and to amortize special tooling costs on low-volume production runs.

29.   In adjusting to the demand for overseas manufacturing and re-export as a necessary condition for marketing in the host country, the international firms have had to increase their commitments of financial and human resources, develop new capabilities for transplanting industrial systems, and adjust their attitude toward ownership and control of overseas affiliates. They have also

14

been faced with the problem of developing local suppliers, providing technical and managerial skills, and upgrading quality control systems to meet international standards. They have had to increase investments in the face of the added risk and uncertainty of doing business in a developing country. Different firms have met this challenge in different ways and with varying degrees of success. Corporate response to these new conditions has depended upon (a) alternative investment and growth opportunities in traditional or home markets and (b) willingness on the part of international firms to take risks and develop new corporate capabilities to manufacture in difficult industrial environments.

## CONDITIONS IN HOME MARKETS

30.    Among European producers, many firms have felt a compelling need to maintain production volumes through exports in order to keep unit costs down. An inadequate domestic market coupled with low levels of protection (the case of Volvo and Saab in Sweden) provides the strongest push into international markets. Passenger car manufacturers have felt the effects of competition for some years now; it is only recently that the cost-profit squeeze induced by increased competition has been felt by truck and tractor producers. In Great Britain and France, a number of firms were unable to replace obsolete equipment and to finance the development of new models. They have been taken over by more successful or by bigger companies. The trend toward national and international mergers is part of the effort to reinforce competitive positions at home and abroad. The major rationale for mergers is: (a) to economize on joint production, distribution, and servicing facilities; (b) to share research and development costs; and (c) to widen access to financial resources.[2]

31.    Pricing in a particular market is based upon the market structure of tariffs, taxes, and competition (not on production costs by international standards). An analysis by *The Economist* dramatizes this point (Annex Table 10). A firm may cut profit margins and absorb additional distribution costs to just above marginal costs in order to maintain production volumes at home and thereby help pay for fixed costs. Thus, Volvo's cars in Germany in 1966 sold for as little as 77 percent of the home country price and Fiats (1500) for

---

[2] Rootes in Great Britain and Simca in France have merged with Chrysler. In the UK, Leyland joined first with Standard-Triumph and then with Rover. B.M.C. took over Jaguar, and finally Leyland took over the B.M.C. successor company to form a single large-scale producing firm (B.L.M.H.). Fiat (Italy) now has some 15 percent of the equity of Citroën (France), and Peugeot, Saviem and Renault have combined operations. In Sweden, Saab and Scania-Vabis have merged.

82 percent. Protection has a pronounced influence in the opposite direction. In Japan, American Mustangs sold for 3.2 times the US price, Fiats (1500) for 1.8 times the Italian price. The indirect effects of protection are also indicated in the set of pricing information provided by a French vehicle manufacturer (Table 2).

TABLE 2:   Price Comparisons, Passenger Vehicles, France and Abroad, 1966

| Country | Firm's Annual Output | Domestic Content (*percent*) | Price Index[a] (*France = 1.0*) |
|---|---|---|---|
| Belgium | 70,000 | 18–19 | 1.0 |
| Spain | 66,000 | 90–94 | 1.3 |
| Algeria | 8,000 | 19–23 | 1.3 |
| Canada | 5,500 | 22–23 | 1.5 |
| Venezuela | 2,600 | 30 | 1.6 |
| Portugal | 2,500 | 28–32 | 1.6 |
| Ireland | 2,000 | 15–20 | 1.6 |
| South Africa | 3,500 | 22–40 | 1.7 |
| Argentina | 24,000 | 97–99 | 2.0 |
| Ivory Coast | 2,500 | 16–18 | 2.0 |
| Morocco | 2,500 | 17–19 | 2.0 |
| Madagascar | 1,200 | 13–15 | 2.0 |
| Brazil | 15,000 | 100 | 2.3 |
| Peru | 1,200 | 10–14 | 3.0 |
| Chile | 600 | 45 | 4.0 |

[a] Converted at official exchange rates, December, 1966.
*Source:* Figures furnished by a French manufacturer.

32.   Tight capital markets and/or restrictions on private foreign investments have inhibited many firms from making the financial investments in manufacturing facilities or distribution and servicing systems necessary to defend overseas markets. International firms encounter difficulties in financing overseas investments because of structural constraints in capital markets, "inadequate" corporate earnings, or restrictions imposed by the government as a result of balance-of-payments problems or political ideology. In Germany, the government supports overseas private investment through long-term capital loans, supplier credits, investment guarantees, and deferred tax payments. In France, limited guarantees of overseas investments linked to exports were introduced in April 1967. In Sweden, the government is opposed in principle to public support of private overseas investment. Balance-of-payments difficulties in the United Kingdom have led to restrictions on private capital transfers outside the developing countries in the sterling area. More recently even the United

16

States has imposed restrictions on overseas investments for balance-of-payments reasons.

33. Labor conditions in the home country are another factor which may influence willingness to locate production facilities abroad. Sweden and Germany are short of industrial labor and have a mild interest in locating production facilities where labor is more plentiful, provided the disadvantages of overseas locations do not offset the labor advantage. Labor-surplus countries such as Finland (7 percent of the labor force is employed in Sweden and elsewhere) and Yugoslavia (large numbers are employed in Germany and Italy) have an interest in the expansion of overseas operations which increase the demand for export of industrial components and parts. For example, Valmet, a farm implement manufacturer in Finland, now sells components and parts to its assembling and manufacturing affiliates in Brazil and Portugal. Similarly a Yugoslav automotive producer, Crvena Zastava, sells components and parts to Egypt, Indonesia, and India.

## CORPORATE ATTITUDES TOWARD OVERSEAS COMMITMENTS

34. The development of an international viewpoint and commitment are critical elements of success or failure in overseas ventures. Many firms, eminently successful in home markets, have been bitterly disappointed abroad. Timing entry of a market is critical. Sufficient resources and capable personnel must be committed to assure the success of the industrial transplant. Smaller firms are less able to man overseas operations than large ones.[3] Some firms have tried to pass off a second-rate product on developing countries; others have failed to devote sufficient resources and personnel for an effective industrial transplant. In many cases, there has been an inbred orientation toward production requirements rather than market opportunities.[4] A dominant corporate attitude that is unreceptive to innovation is also a basic hindrance.[5]

---

[3] A Swedish manufacturer estimated that 17 people from the home office were needed to run a truck manufacturing plant in Brazil, and recruiting for these critical positions was very difficult (see also para. 53).

[4] Many firms chose to give up overseas markets rather than disrupt the home operation. See, for example, reference to a British firm's attitudes in "British Motor Corporation: The Commercial Crunch," *The Economist* (November 26, 1966). See also Igor Ansoff, *Corporate Strategy: An Analytic Approach to Business Policy for Growth and Expansion* (New York, 1965), pp. 41, 104–108.

[5] Richard N. Farmer and Barry M. Richman, *Comparative Management and Economic Progress* (Homewood, Illinois, 1965), pp. 208 ff.

17

35. The trend toward overseas manufacturing has increased the capital investment required to maintain or expand a firm's share of the world market. This includes investments in marketing and distribution systems, in engineering and design capabilities, and in overseas physical plants. Firms anxious to secure overseas contracts have often ended up in a cost-profit squeeze, especially where price ceilings have prevailed or demand has fallen short of expectations. The latter was the case of Berliet in Algeria, and it contributed to Fiat's demise in Mexico. Citroën lost money in Argentina until it was able to cut prices to the point where increased demand allowed it to bring production to a profitable level. A basic dilemma is that in order to be competitive it is necessary to maintain a diversified product line, which increases capital requirements and undermines efforts to maintain volume in production runs. Berliet, the largest truck manufacturer in France (18,000 a year), was forced into marginal pricing of trucks and sub-assemblies in order to maintain production volume at home. (See also para. 46D.) A small producer such as FSA (Fiat-France, formerly a part of Simca), which manufactured 6,000 trucks and 12,000 tractors in 1966, had to maintain 30 variations in truck models based upon four different engines and five combinations of axle-and-gear systems. Engines were supplied by Fiat from Italy. In the passenger car field, Volkswagen and Volvo have managed to do well with a much narrower product range.

36. In those overseas markets where manufacturing has become a requirement, the most successful firms have been those that have been willing to adjust operations and develop the necessary capabilities to effect transplants. For example, Massey-Ferguson, one of the world's leading tractor manufacturers, completely reorganized their management system to handle overseas plants in the "nursery stage." They have developed this type of business to the point where 15 percent of company earnings is derived from developing countries, as compared to 2 to 3 percent for some other international firms. At Fiat, a separate division handles the shipment of knocked-down units to overseas manufacturing affiliates, which now account for 10 percent of total sales.

## INVESTMENT RISKS AND "ADEQUATE" EARNINGS

37. International firms become involved in overseas ventures in different forms and with varying degrees of resource commitment. These forms range from licensing arrangements to full ownership and control of an overseas manufacturing affiliate. Resource commitment may range from a few technical experts on a reimbursable fee basis to substantial commitments of financial and other corporate resources. Where resource commitment is involved,

the international firm must take into account: (a) the long-term prospect for earning a return, (b) the availability of financial and other resources, (c) the relative risk and uncertainty in a particular venture, and (d) alternative opportunities to earn profits. Added risk and uncertainty are weighed against the chance of a quick return and the prospect of being shut out of future market opportunities.

38. International corporations earn a return on overseas ventures from: (a) royalty and licensing fees, (b) return on equity, and (c) sale of sub-assemblies and equipment, which include replacement components and parts. Some firms prefer equity participation in order to maximize returns and to assure adequate managerial control. Others are less inclined and less able to risk capital and prefer licensing arrangements, which often yield substantial returns in the form of royalties and profits on sale of sub-assemblies. Inflation and exchange fluctuation are the two major factors that intensify the risk and uncertainty of realizing an adequate return, maintaining the value of invest-ments, and remitting profits. Investment requirements depend in part upon existing supplier capability and the degree of autarky imposed by the govern-ment. Most firms try to minimize capital commitments. In some countries, they are able to hedge on currencies liable to devaluation, but this increases opera-tional costs. (See also para. 66.)

39. Many firms expect a higher-than-normal return in developing countries where the political or economic risks are higher. The risks they are willing to take are in part determined by how satisfactorily they are doing in traditional markets and whether the firm is making a special effort to extend its share of world markets. Much also depends upon the size of the firm and its ability to commit resources to relatively small earnings bases scattered throughout the world. Some firms count on a quick return in the first 2 to 4 years, before domestic manufacturing requirements and intensified foreign exchange restric-tions imposed in the developing country begin to narrow profits. Some of these firms have been overoptimistic in their evaluations and have encountered a variety of difficulties either in realizing an adequate return or in remitting their profits.

40. Substantial portions of an international firm's earnings come from the sale of components and parts to original equipment manufacturers and to the replacement market. Their investments in overseas manufacturing facilities are in a sense an investment in future demand for components and parts. For example, Leyland can afford to earn a small return on buses, because these earnings are offset by profitable returns on an expanding demand for Leyland

engines and spare parts. Some firms (Renault and Fiat) also earn substantial amounts from technical services and on the sale of specialized equipment for parts manufacture.[6]

41. Royalties must generally be kept to a minimum because of political considerations and remittance problems. To counter this, prices on knocked-down vehicles and parts are often set high to offset the possibility of future restrictions on royalties or in the event of unforeseen increases in production costs. For example, one firm had to run special body panels for hand-welding in the overseas assembly plant.

## OWNERSHIP AND CONTROL OF OVERSEAS AFFILIATES

42. Issues over ownership and control depend upon: (a) the nature of arrangements with the manufacturing affiliate, (b) corporate policy, and (c) the host government's attitude toward foreign investment. In the case of joint ventures, ownership has a bearing upon profits and technical control of the manufacturing operation. For the investor, majority control assures wider latitude and flexibility on: (a) inter-company pricing, (b) reinvestment of profits for future growth, and (c) managerial control over manufacturing operations to maintain international standards on product and trade names. Technical control is critical if there are to be plans for an international manufacture and interchange system. Under licensing arrangements, the return is based on the licensing fee and profits from the sale of parts. Aside from trade name considerations, the licensor without equity investment has a limited interest in the commercial viability of the overseas venture.

43. In the case of joint ventures, attitudes of the host government toward majority participation of the foreign partner are critical. Fundamentally, this is a matter of political ideology, particularly in the early process of national development. Mexico and India have been especially insistent upon majority control by nationals, although both governments recognize the benefits derived

---

[6] For some insights on the "irrationality" of foreign investment decisions, see Yair Ahoroni, *The Foreign Investment Decision Process* (1966), pp. 49–75. Among the reasons cited for looking abroad are: fear of losing the market; the bandwagon effect; strong competition from abroad in the home market; and creation of a market for sale of components or other return on know-how and research. Organizational evolution at top management levels from a basically domestic orientation to a multinational one is a critical element of the firm's operational efficiency overseas. This reorientation profoundly affects the firm's attitude toward risk-taking in unfamiliar areas, *op. cit.*, pp. 173–198.

from foreign capital and know-how.[7] For one thing, most governments realize that exchange costs for foreign equity participation may be more costly in the long run. More basically, it is an understandable matter of national pride to keep domestic industry in the hands of nationals.

44.    Attitudes toward ownership and control vary from one corporation to another. General Motors, and more recently Ford, have insisted upon 100 percent ownership; Chrysler, a newcomer, has been much more flexible and willing even to accept minority interest. Chrysler's acceptance in countries like Mexico and India is in part a reflection of its willingness to hold a minority interest. Permissiveness in licensing arrangements depends in part upon the relative technological lead a firm has over its affiliate. For example, Massey-Ferguson and Cummins Engine both invest considerable resources in research and development of products and techniques and are not too concerned about a licensee in a developing country eventually gaining the upper hand as a market competitor.[8] This would be less true of a licensor with a more stable, less sophisticated technology. Many governments would much prefer purchasing know-how outright, rather than accepting foreign equity investment, but foreign partners often feel they will not be able to earn an adequate return on a license basis.

---

[7] On the difficulties of doing business in India, see Jack Baranson, *Manufacturing Problems in India* (Syracuse University Press, 1967), pp. 49–53. The detrimental economic effects of assimilation policies are pointed out in Harry G. Johnson, "A Theoretical Model of Economic Nationalism in New and Developing States," *Political Science Quarterly*, LXXX, No. 2 (June 1965), pp. 169–185.

[8] This, of course, is not the case in licensing arrangements with firms in industrially-advanced countries, where future marketing rights are more rigidly controlled. The Cummins case is documented in Baranson, *Manufacturing Problems in India*, p. 24.

# IV

## ADAPTATION PROBLEMS OF
## MANUFACTURING AFFILIATES

45.   Problems of adjustment are, first, inherent in the production techniques of automotive products, and secondly, derive from the differences in production environments encountered in small-scale or developing economies. The products themselves can be ill-suited to consumer needs or physical environments of another country. Among the major deficiencies in operating manufacturing plants are underdeveloped supplier capacities, inadequate quality control systems, and a dearth of qualified technicians and managers. By creating a "sellers' market," protection and import substitution tend to undermine quality and reliability. Government systems of industrial licensing and resource allocation, which includes import control, compound the difficulties of scheduling production and add to production costs. Delays of a year or more to obtain an import license and to deliver goods are not unusual.

### RELEVANT CHARACTERISTICS OF
### AUTOMOTIVE PRODUCTION

46.   The nature of automotive products and their production techniques have an important influence on the economics of industrialization in developing economies. The following aspects are relevant:

A. *Vast range of components and parts.* There are literally thousands of elements that go into a single vehicle. A small British car averages 2,500 major parts and assemblies, or 20,000 parts if every nut and bolt is counted separately. A standard diesel engine consists of 750 parts provided by about 200 different plants. About 15,000 separate machining and treatment processes are required to turn steel shapes, forgings, and castings into finished engine components such as pistons and engine blocks.[1] When one multiplies the requirements for a single vehicle by the number of vehicle models and configurations required by small economies, the burden upon component and part manufacturers appears formidable.

B. *Complexity of specifications and standards.* Components and parts are manufactured from hundreds of different types of iron and steel and other industrial metals and materials including rubber, plastic and glass. Mass production of standardized components and parts demands rigid uniformity in materials specifications and manufacturing tolerances. High engineering and managerial skills are required to ensure the necessary quality and reliability in components and parts.

C. *Production techniques.* Mechanization and automation are associated with the high-volume techniques that are used to manufacture all but a limited range of specialized vehicles and parts in plants producing for large domestic or world markets. Automated transfer lines (including rearrangeable standard machine elements) reduce operating and handling costs, increase the rate of utilization of expensive equipment, and reduce costs for machine tools, factory space, rejected parts, and machine maintenance. But in plants serving limited domestic markets, these more efficient techniques are precluded because of the low volume of the market. It is the diseconomies of small-scale production that contribute most to the high costs of local manufacture. By contrast continuous-flow techniques associated with high-volume production also pose formidable problems of manpower skills and industrial logistics for newly industrializing countries.[2] Thus there is a dilemma in the choice of industrial techniques—between highly integrated and mechanized equipment requiring sophisticated engineering and managerial control and less mechanized or automated equipment requiring the higher machine skills and technical personnel to convert and adapt techniques.[3]

---

[1] See George Maxcy and Aubrey Silberston, "Techniques of Production," *The Motor Industry* (London, 1959), pp. 53–61; and Baranson, *Manufacturing Problems in India*, p. 19.

[2] See David Granick, *Soviet Metal-Fabricating and Economic Development* (University of Wisconsin Press, 1967), pp. 25–27, 115–119.

[3] Japan has had considerable success in utilizing small-scale parts manufacturers who employ labor at lower wages and use less sophisticated machine tools. But unlike India, Japan has the engineers and technicians to convert techniques and a skilled labor force to compensate for quality and control that is not built into the machine. See Baranson, *Manufacturing Problems in India*, pp. 68–69. (See also para. 57.)

D. *Minimum scale and optimum technique.* Choices in techniques of production depend largely upon the vehicle series and the degree of autarky enforced in the economy. High volume, automated techniques are associated with standard model passenger cars and light trucks with interrelated production runs of anywhere between 100,000 and 500,000 a year or more. Thresholds for economic scale production drop to from 20,000 to 40,000 on medium-size trucks (3 to 8 tons) and to 5,000 or less on more specialized medium and heavy trucks and buses. A medium truck manufacturer such as Berliet has to offer anywhere from 70 to 200 combinations of engine, transmission, chassis, and load-carrying frame to compete in its field. Economies of scale are more pronounced in metal stamping and in the forging or machining of parts where mechanized or automated equipment can be used, than in assembly or finishing operations requiring a minimum of machine tools or equipment.

## SUITABILITY OF PRODUCT DESIGN

47. In transferring automotive production to developing countries, international firms have kept adjustments in product design and production techniques to a minimum. This is because such adjustments are costly and disrupt the industrial transplant process. But from the viewpoint of the developing economy, there is great potential advantage in making automotive products that are more closely adapted to local market demands and operational environments. For example, in developing countries where crop yields per acre are low, harvesting combines require "big mouths and small stomachs"; in agricultural sectors with higher crop yields, the need is for "small mouths and big stomachs." Climatic differences, terrain, and differences among crops also necessitate design variations in the harvester's "pickup" mechanism. Another example relates to commercial trucks operating in economies with acute capital scarcity. Small trucking companies in Japan that are short of working capital prefer to purchase equipment with a shorter operating life and higher operational costs, rather than incur high initial capital outlays.[4]

48. For products to be manufactured in the developing country, there is a further need to adapt product design and manufacturing techniques to the smaller market volumes and more limited production capabilities typically encountered in developing countries. Thus Chrysler found it necessary to build

---

[4] The economic costs of a truck engine will depend upon product weight, horsepower, engine life, engine reliability, and fuel consumption. These characteristics in turn are decided by the regulations governing truck loads, highway speeds, and the physical conditions of roads (including average grades and surfacing). *Ibid.*, pp. 27–33.

25 percent more value into Turkish trucks (axles, shock absorbers, and differentials) in order to withstand local road conditions and driver usage. A British electrical automotive parts firm designed a high frequency horn for trucks sold in the Indian market because of differences in local traffic conditions. In Argentina, as in many other developing countries, bus bodies are built locally for truck chassis manufactured by Mercedes to cater to the variety of local preferences.

## DEVELOPING QUALITY STANDARDS AND SUPPLIER CAPABILITIES

49. It is important for the developing countries to achieve and maintain quality standards in the production of basic materials for the manufacture of intermediate components and the assembly of finished vehicles. This is an especially difficult task in economies sheltered from competitive forces, since inferior quality can undermine the entire fabric of production and indirectly contribute to even higher production costs than a comparison of market prices would indicate. Many basic materials that are considered standard stock in open economies often must be procured locally or specially ordered in small batches at considerably higher cost or at inferior quality. Moreover, reliability in product standards is a fundamental requirement for trading in international markets, where major growth opportunities may lie.[5] The foreign licensor has a major role in developing standards and specifications and in establishing quality control procedures, but success ultimately depends upon the attitude and commitment of local management.

50. Obtaining basic materials according to required specifications is a major difficulty in economies that are only able to support a limited range of industrial activities. There are approximately 300 different materials of varying shapes and specifications in a standard diesel truck engine. Lack of uniformity in raw materials and semifinished goods such as castings and forgings creates special problems in milling and machining to required specifications.[6] In high-volume production, precision and uniformity are built into automated equip-

---

[5] A major ingredient of Japan's postwar success in supplying world markets with engineering products stems from the emphasis Japanese industrialists placed upon quality control. This emphasis stands in marked contrast to countries like India, where plant engineers will argue that an industrial product such as a diesel engine which falls substantially short of international standards is "good enough" for India. *Ibid.*, pp. 78–79.

[6] Porosity (air-bubbles in castings) is a typical problem which required 100 percent inspection procedures after milling to assure rejection of substandard parts. Rejection rates on defective parts in India have averaged three to four times those in the United States in certain cases. *Ibid.*, pp. 78–79.

ment. Developing countries with limited markets are much more dependent upon the very machine labor skills in which they are deficient. They also lack the engineers and technicians to correct machine-intensive techniques for differences in factor costs and proficiencies.

51. Supplier industries are crucial in the development of an automotive industry. Typical procurement items are forgings, castings, brakes, pistons, bearings, suspension springs, gaskets, bolts, and all types of electrical equipment and instruments. Outside plant procurement averages about 60 percent by value in industrially-advanced economies, as compared to only 40 percent in countries like Mexico and Brazil, where supplier industries are not as well developed. The higher percentage of in-plant production intensifies the diseconomies of small-scale production. Given the foreign exchange constraints under which developing economies are attempting to industrialize, vehicle manufacturers are under relentless pressure to develop local suppliers of components and parts. The manufacturer-supplier relationship in developing economies is the exact reverse of what is typical of industrialized areas, where the manufacturer relies upon supplier know-how even to design required components and parts. In developing areas, it is the other way around; licensors have a heavy responsibility to help develop the supplier industry, which even in countries like Mexico and Brazil typically lacks engineering capability and foreign contacts.[7]

52. Many of the larger automotive manufacturers in industrially advanced countries own subsidiaries to manufacture strategically important parts such as axles, crankshafts, bearings, and engines, because of their special manufacturing requirements. These subsidiaries specialize and sell to other manufacturers as well. But vertical integration is practiced to a much higher degree in developing countries than in industrialized economies. Kaiser reports that in the United States they depend upon outside suppliers for transmission and engine components, but this was not the case in Brazil and Argentina. Both Willys-Overland of Brazil and Industrias Kaiser Argentina are highly integrated companies with their own engine, axle and transmission plants, foundry and forge facilities, body stamping plants, and tool and die facilities. This degree of vertical integration was considered necessary to assure an adequate supply and acceptable quality of components in the newly developing automotive sectors.

---

[7] For a description of the role of vehicle manufacturers in developing local supplier capacities, see Guillermo S. Edelberg, *The Procurement Practices of the Mexican Affiliates of Selected United States Automobile Firms* (doctoral thesis, Harvard University, 1964).

# MANPOWER DEFICIENCIES

53.  Plants in developing economies are especially short of managerial and supervisory personnel to transmit technology and carry on plant operations. This includes engineering, financial, and marketing people to plan, organize, and carry out a production program. There is an even more acute shortage of "conversion" engineers to adapt product designs and production techniques to local environments and deficiencies. Organization and management is especially critical in automotive manufacturing operations involving tens of thousands of parts and hundreds of suppliers. Plant engineering, quality control, production and cost control (including the preparation of production standards and machine-load studies), and inventory control are among the many specialties in which experienced personnel are difficult to find. Volkswagen was especially outspoken on the shortage of such people ("fachleute"), complaining that engineers from developing countries often lacked the necessary practical experience to take over plant responsibilities and are often unwilling to soil their hands in factories. Typically, there was an inadequate supply of the 20 to 30 middle-range managers, technical supervisors, and master mechanics necessary to set up initial procedures and improvise or make adjustments when things went wrong, especially during the first years of plant run-in.

# V

---

# COST COMPARISONS

---

54. There are considerable differences in the costs of production in developing and small-scale economies operating under varying degrees of protection on the one hand and those in economies subject to international competition on the other. The data analyzed in this chapter reveal ex-factory costs averaging between 60 and 150 percent higher among the major automotive producers in Latin America (Brazil, Mexico, and Argentina) than in the United States. In India, ex-factory prices on passenger cars in a low volume series with an 85 percent domestic content, were 120 percent above the ex-factory price of a comparable vehicle manufactured in Europe under high volume conditions. High domestic content[1] (60 to 90 percent) of components and parts produced at relatively low volumes in small-scale plants is a major contributor to high

---

[1] The definition of domestic content varies widely depending upon the country and the particular interpretation of regulations and administrative decrees. In most instances, domestic content is based upon vehicle value, but in some countries it is computed on the basis of weight. (One of the problems in negotiating interchange agreements in the Latin American Free Trade Area is reconciling value and weight systems.) Import authorizations under a value system are usually calculated from the *c.i.f.* price of an equivalent import without duty. Incentive provisions of automotive decrees are often in terms of meeting a minimum domestic content. Administrative interpretation varies over (a) what may be included in value added by the firm, (b) what percentage of locally purchased parts may be considered as domestic content, and (c) the degree to which taxes or duties are included in direct or indirect domestic content. See also footnote 9.

costs. Internationally, production costs per unit level off at about 120,000 units per year on assembly operations, 240,000 for engines and other power train parts, and 600,000 units for body stampings—scales achieved only by the largest of the international firms. The major production cost economies are realized as production approaches these levels. In developing countries the highest production volumes are one-tenth of this figure. Cost differences may be accounted for by factor price distortions, low-volume production, and/or excess profits. These in turn are attributable to a protected market structure and related tariff and exchange policies.[2] Aside from these market structure limits, there is the factor of technical efficiency, which includes optimality in plant design and operation.

## ANALYSIS OF COMPARATIVE COST DATA

55.   Cost differences in a particular country depend upon the nature and degree of these technical and economic inefficiencies, and upon the stage reached in the learning process. The number of plants authorized to manufacture vehicles and the proliferation of models and makes both have a strong bearing upon the size of production runs and the relative diseconomies of scale. The scope and pace of industrialization also have an indirect effect upon sector efficiency. In several countries, the drive toward autarky in a wide range of industrial activities simultaneously has strained human resources and existing capabilities to organize and carry out production programs and maintain quality standards, thereby contributing indirectly to the increased costs of production.

56.   In the material that follows, two sets of comparative domestic production cost data are presented, one for India and another for Latin America. The cost curves for India (Chart 1) are for passenger cars. They show cost increments over time for a single firm with increases in domestic content and at output levels varying between 3,000 to 12,000 vehicles per year. The Latin American data (Chart 2 and related tables) provide inter-country comparisons for light vehicles manufactured in Argentina, Brazil and Mexico. (See also the cost analysis of the New Zealand industry, paras. 108–110.) In applying the sets of data presented in Charts 1 and 2, it should be remembered that the

---

[2] Cost comparisons are based upon conversions at the official exchange rate at the time, unless otherwise noted. On the intricacy of exchange valuations, see paragraph 57 including footnote 4. Costs in all countries (including the USA) are here defined to include any effect of tariffs and indirect taxes on all inputs. They are the *actual* costs to the manufacturer.

CHART 1
INCREASE IN PRODUCTION COSTS AS A FUNCTION OF DOMESTIC
CONTENT AND PRODUCTION VOLUME PASSENGER CAR—INDIA, 1966

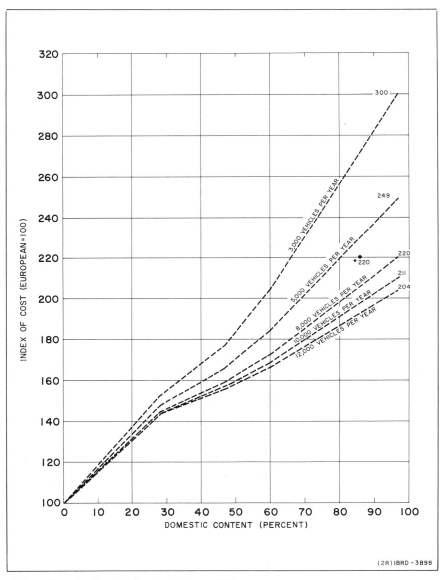

\* Actual production, April 1966 (5,700 vehicles per year).
*Source:* See Annex Table 9.

CHART 2

MANUFACTURING COSTS IN LATIN AMERICA AS A FUNCTION OF
DOMESTIC CONTENT, JANUARY 1967

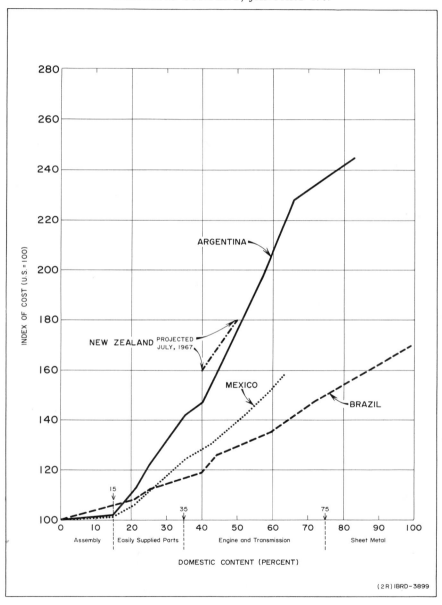

*Source:* See Tables 3, 4 and 5.

31

cost curves relate to a particular type of vehicle, a particular firm, a particular economy, and a particular point in time. The following should also be noted:

(i) Costs to the firm vary with: (a) the percentage of in-plant production, (b) the scale of plant, and (c) capacity utilization. These variables are indirectly affected by the size of the industrial economy and the stage of development which have a profound effect upon the cost decisions to make or buy particular components or parts.

(ii) Data apply to a given number of model variations in an industrial complex turning out other series and models. Proliferation in the product mix, without proportional increases in overall volume, would shift the curves upward.

(iii) Domestic price structure, taxes, tariffs, and the exchange rate vary over time. Costs of domestic procurement, which loom large in the production bill, are influenced by obtainable profits of component and materials suppliers under noncompetitive conditions and by their relative efficiency. Tax (or tariff) increases or a lagging exchange rate would shift cost curves upward. Devaluation, not offset by subsequent increases in domestic prices and production costs, would shift the curves downward.

(iv) Costs reflect a particular point on the firm's learning curve. Improvements in plant efficiency, other factors remaining unchanged, would result in a downward shift in the cost curves. The same applies to capacity utilization, which may vary over time. It has not been possible to separate cost differences attributable to diseconomies of small-scale production and those due to learning, but it would be very useful and significant to do so.[3]

---

[3] There are several possibilities. One would be to use as a benchmark of efficiency a comparable plant in a more advanced stage of learning. Another approach would be to study a single plant over an extended learning period during which its production volume had remained stable. Learning curve concepts applied to an industrial sector are the basis of the infant industry argument first expounded by Friedrich List and Mihail Manoilesco. Both advocated protective tariffs to transfer labor from low-productivity agriculture to more productive industry. The classical infant industry argument refers largely to the development of external and internal economies of scale with market growth over time. Little has been added to the concept since it was advanced more than 35 years ago. From an economic standpoint, infant industries are justifiable where the added costs of protection are eventually compensated by added national income, where costs exceed social costs due to taxes or price distortions, or where the social returns sufficiently exceed private returns.

# INDIA

57. In India prior to the June 1966 devaluation, production costs for passenger cars ran about 2.2 times those in Europe (see below and Chart 1). This was for a Fiat-type vehicle at very low volume (about 5,700 vehicles a year) and high national content (about 85 percent). The Indian plant also manufactured two models of small and medium-size trucks—with a total output of just over 12,000 units annually. The 2.2 cost comparison was as of April 1966, just before the rupee was devalued by about 60 percent (from Rs 4.76 = $1.00 to Rs 7.50 = $1.00). Ex-factory domestic prices increased 11 percent following devaluation. This meant that immediately following devaluation the Indian prices were 1.6 times the ex-factory European prices. It is difficult to foretell at the time of writing what the net effect of devaluation will be.[4]

| Ex-factory price of a passenger car | India | Europe | Ratio |
|---|---|---|---|
| Before devaluation | Rs 11,320 | Rs 5,118 | 2.2 |
| After devaluation | Rs 12,664 | Rs 8,064 | 1.6 |

58. Another Indian manufacturer of heavy (eight-ton) trucks reported price competitiveness with the producer of the comparable European model. The Indian export price was actually 6 percent below the comparable European product immediately following devaluation, as compared to 23 percent above prior to devaluation. But this was on a series where volume was much closer to European standards—about 19,000 in India as compared to 30,000 in Europe. (See also para. 139.)

| Ex-factory price, 8-ton truck | India | Europe | Ratio |
|---|---|---|---|
| Before devaluation | Rs 30,000 | Rs 24,800 | 1.23 |
| After devaluation | Rs 35,200[a] | Rs 37,600[b] | 0.94 |

[a] This is the Indian price excluding domestic sales tax, which amounts to Rs 10,000 on a vehicle of this type. The price does include about Rs 5,000 in custom duties and raw materials tax.

[b] Allowances have been made for differences in the European and Indian model. In addition to this, the dealer's commission in India is about half that in Europe (5.2 percent, or Rs 1,800, as compared to 12.5 percent, or Rs 4,700 in Europe).

---

[4] Actually, the full inflationary effect that one would normally expect as a result of devaluation was considerably dampened by the recession that began in late 1966. The average growth rate in the industrial sector dropped from 8 percent to 2 percent— textiles and capital goods were particularly hard hit. Declines in the capital goods industry resulted from a drop in the level of aggregate demand in both the public and private sectors. Budgetary constraints have forced cutbacks in equipment procurement contracts. Because of the recession, the demand for imports lagged behind available

TABLE 3: Comparison of Internal Costs, Cars and Light Trucks, Argentina, Brazil, Mexico and USA, January 1967

(US$ equivalents)

| | Latin American Costs[a] | | | | | US Costs | | | | Ratios | | |
|---|---|---|---|---|---|---|---|---|---|---|---|---|
| | Domestic Value Added at Market Prices (1) | C.i.f. Value of Imported Content[b] (2) | Ex-factory (3) (1) + (2) | Taxes[c] (4) | Cost Net of Taxes (5) (3) − (4) | Ex-factory[d] (6) | Net of Taxes[e] (7) | C.i.f. Latin America[f] (8) | Foreign Exchange Savings (9) (8) − (2) | Ex-factory Latin America USA (10) (3) ÷ (6) | Cost of Domestic Value Added[g] (11) (1) ÷ (9) | Resource Costs Net of Taxes Latin America USA (12) (5) ÷ (7) |
| *Argentina:* | | | | | | | | | | | | |
| Car | $4,244 | $ 371 | $4,615 | $1,463 | $3,152 | $1,775 | $1,573 | $2,475 | $2,104 | 2.60 | 2.02 | 2.00 |
| Light Truck | 3,476 | 593 | 4,069 | 1,290 | 2,779 | 1,634 | 1,448 | 2,469 | 1,876 | 2.50 | 1.85 | 1.92 |
| *Brazil:* | | | | | | | | | | | | |
| Light Truck | 2,841 | 155 | 2,996 | 1,013 | 1,983 | 1,752 | 1,552 | 2,587 | 2,432 | 1.71 | 1.17 | 1.28 |
| *Mexico:* | | | | | | | | | | | | |
| Car (small) | 1,902 | 978 | 2,880 | 311 | 2,569 | 1,756 | 1,556 | 1,956 | 978 | 1.64 | 1.95 | 1.65 |
| Car (large) | 2,564 | 1,203 | 3,767 | 407 | 3,360 | 2,297 | 2,035 | 2,497 | 1,294 | 1.64 | 1.98 | 1.65 |
| Light Truck | 1,728 | 902 | 2,630 | 284 | 2,346 | 1,604 | 1,421 | 1,804 | 902 | 1.64 | 1.92 | 1.65 |

[a] Cost in local currency converted to dollars at official exchange rate at time of procurement. (In the case of Argentina, this was prior to devaluation in March 1967, or 250 pesos = US$1.00.) Figures for annual production runs of 20,000 to 30,000 vehicles—which is 5 to 10 percent the size of production for comparable vehicles in the USA.

[b] These figures, calculated from base figures given in column 8, include allowances for import content of domestically supplied parts (estimated at 15 percent for Argentina, 30 percent for Mexico, and 10 percent for Brazil).

[c] Roughly 31.9 percent of manufacturing price in Argentina, 33.8 percent in Brazil, and 10.8 percent in Mexico.

[d] Cost estimate for a "reconstituted" vehicle equivalent to the overseas model.

[e] Based on estimated average of 11.4 percent. This includes all Federal, State and Local taxes (corporate income, excise and social security). A comparable concept is used in estimating tax component for the Latin American countries.

[f] Difference between "C.i.f. Latin America" (column 8) and "US ex-factory", (column 6) Latin America" (column 8) and "US ex-factory", it does *not* include import duties.

[g] This is akin to the "Bruno ratio." See Bruno, *op. cit*, p. 109.

*Source:* Calculated from data furnished by an American vehicle manufacturer.

34

59.   An earlier study on diesel engine manufacture in India reveals two basic causes of high cost structure in that country: (a) a much smaller scale of production relative to internationally competitive plants, and (b) high procurement costs of materials and parts also produced in small-scale plants under a protectionist regime.[5] It cost nearly three times as much to produce a diesel engine in India as it did in the United States (Annex Table 11). Although direct labor cost 0.6 as much, procured materials and parts, which constituted 75 percent of the engine value, cost 3.3 times their US equivalents (then at Rs 4.75 to the dollar).

## ARGENTINA, BRAZIL AND MEXICO

60.   In the analysis that follows, production costs for a small car, a large car and a light truck made by the same international manufacturing firm in Argentina, Brazil and Mexico are compared to those in the United States. The same set of data is broken down in three ways. Table 3 compares domestic ex-factory costs with import costs and then compares costs net of taxes to arrive at the difference in resource costs. Table 4 analyzes cost increments as a function of domestic content. Table 5 compares the cost elements of labor, materials, and indirect charges.

61.   The ex-factory cost of light truck manufacture runs 2.5 times US costs in Argentina,[6] 1.7 times in Brazil, and 1.6 times in Mexico (Table 3, column 10). Cost differences for passenger cars are about the same; aside from obvious body differences, there is a close similarity in the production of light trucks and passenger cars both in terms of components and parts and length of production runs (para. 16). Column 11 gives domestic resource costs per dollar of foreign exchange savings—which is akin to the "Bruno ratio" or the shadow rate of exchange.[7] Thus, for Argentine cars, it cost $4,244 (pesos converted at official rate at the time of procurement, column 1) to produce foreign exchange

foreign exchange at a time when, as a result of import liberalization, import licenses became easier to get. Because of severe import restrictions prior to the devaluation, many firms are now importing in excess of their actual needs as a hedge against a recurring foreign exchange shortage. Once the recession is over, renewed demand for foreign exchange coupled with revived internal demand for goods may raise domestic prices and narrow the competitive price advantages initially gained from devaluation. (See Baranson, *Manufacturing Problems in India*, pp. 127—128.)

[5] *Ibid.*, p. 88.

[6] See also cost comparison in Chapter VI on Argentina, paras. 79 and 80.

[7] See Michael Bruno, *Inter-dependence, Resource Use and Structural Change in Trade* (Jerusalem, 1963), pp. 104—113. This ratio is closely related to the concept of effective protection, which is defined as the extent by which domestic value added (measured in domestic prices) exceeds value added at world prices.

**TABLE 4:  Cost Increases at Successive Stages of Local Integration in Production of Cars and Light Trucks, Argentina, Brazil and Mexico, January 1967**

| Component Groupings | Argentina | | | | Brazil | | | | Mexico | | | | Relative Investment Needed per Dollar of Parts Production[b] |
|---|---|---|---|---|---|---|---|---|---|---|---|---|---|
| | Cost Index[a] ($US=100$) | Share of Total Content % | Contribution to Cost Increase ($US\ total=100$) | Cumulative Index of Cost Increases ($US\ total=100$) | Cost Index[a] ($US=100$) | Share of Total Content % | Contribution to Cost Increase ($US\ total=100$) | Cumulative Index of Cost Increases ($US\ total=100$) | Cost Index ($US=100$) | Share of Total Content % | Contribution to Cost Increase ($US\ total=100$) | Cumulative Index of Cost Increases ($US\ total=100$) | |
| | (1) | (2) | (3) $(1)\times(2)$ | (4) | (5) | (6) | (7) $(5)\times(6)$ | (8) | (9) | (10) | (11) $(9)\times(10)$ | (12) | (13) |
| *Local Content* | | | | | | | | | | | | | |
| 1. Assembly items | 115 | 15 | 17 | 102 | 140 | 15 | 21 | 106 | 106 | 15 | 16 | 101 | 4 |
| 2. Mandatory items | 280 | 6 | 17 | 113 | 150 | 6 | 9 | 109 | 180 | 6 | 11 | 106 | 1 |
| 3. Easily supplied parts | 320 | 4 | 13 | 122 | 160 | 4 | 7 | 112 | 225 | 4 | 9 | 111 | 2 |
| 4. Supplier development required | 300 | 10 | 30 | 142 | 150 | 10 | 15 | 117 | 230 | 10 | 23 | 124 | 3 |
| 5. Engine & driveline-assembly and machinery | | | | | | | | | | | | | |
|   a. –Make | 190 | 5 | 10 | 147 | 130 | 5 | 7 | 119 | 190 | 6 | 11 | 129 | |
|   b. –Buy | 400 | 3 | 12 | 156 | 270 | 4 | 11 | 126 | 240 | 1 | 2 | 130 | 6 |
| 6. Engine & driveline-foundry | | | | | | | | | | | | | |
|   a. –Make | 400 | 14 | 56 | 198 | 160 | 13 | 21 | 134 | 220 | 10 | 22 | 142 | 5 |
|   b. –Buy | | | | | 180 | 3 | 5 | 136 | | | | | |
| 7. Amortization and running costs of parts requiring specialized investment | 430 | 9 | 39 | 228 | 200 | 12 | 24 | 148 | 240 | 8 | 19 | 153 | 7 |
| 8. Sheet metal & other components | 200 | 17 | 34 | 245 | 180 | 27 | 49 | 170 | 250 | 3 | 8 | 158 | 8 |
| 9. Subtotal | 272[c] | 83 | 227 | 245 | 172[c] | 99 | 169 | 170 | 192[c] | 63 | 121 | 158 | |
| 10. Import Content | 161[d] | 17 | 27 | 254 | 160[d] | 1 | 2 | 171 | 115[d] | 37 | 43 | | |
| 11. Total Vehicle | 254 | 100 | 254 | 254 | 171 | 100 | 171 | 171 | 164 | 100 | 164 | 164 | |

[a] Compares manufacturing costs for cars and light trucks (see Table 3, column 10 and footnote a). Computation of indices is explained in note below.

[b] Investments ranked from lowest (1) to highest (8). Investment costs of supplier firms are *not* included.

[c] Derived from line 9, columns 2 and 3, 6 and 7, 10 and 11.

[d] Includes import duty on residual items.

*Note:* This table illustrates costs of vehicle production in selected Latin American countries as compared with production costs in the United States. Column (1) shows the index of increased costs at each production stage as compared with US costs. Column (2) indicates the percentage value of local content to the total vehicle for each production stage. Column (3) indicates the cost increase for each production stage: i.e., column (1) × column (2). Column (4) gives average total costs at each successive stage of production. For example, on line 2 under Argentina, 15 percent total content is produced locally at 15 percent (column 1) more than US ex-factory costs (from line 1), 6 percent total content is produced locally at 180 percent (column 1) more than US ex-factory costs. At this stage, if the remaining 79 percent (100–15–6) is valued at US ex-factory costs, the result would be 113 (line 2, column 4), computed as follows: .15(115) + .06(280) + .79(100) = 113. The cumulative cost index for the Argentine vehicle is 254 (line 10, column 4). In other words, a vehicle which costs $2,000 to manufacture in the US, would cost $5,080 to reproduce in Argentina.

*Source:* Calculated from data furnished by an American vehicle manufacturer.

savings of \$2,104 (column 9)—a ratio of 2.02 (column 11). This means a peso valued at 250 to the US dollar at the time of procurement would have to be valued at 505 to the US dollar (250 times 2.02) to equate the difference in resource costs. For a comparison of relative *resource* costs, estimated indirect taxes have been subtracted from ex-factory costs to obtain the ratios shown in column 12. Relative to the US tax incidence, taxes in Argentina and Brazil are substantially higher and in Mexico slightly lower.[8] The competitive position in world markets lies somewhere between the two ratios shown in column 10 and 12, depending on how the tax component is evaluated.

62.   Table 4 breaks down the manufacturing costs for light trucks in Latin America, while Chart 2 shows manufacturing cost increases as a function of domestic content[9] for annual production runs of between 20,000 and 30,000 vehicles per year. These cost indices not only reflect the increased costs of domestic manufacture in the numerator, they are also net of the so-called deletion allowance given by the overseas supplier. The deletion allowances are characteristically well below proportional shares of *c.i.f.* prices.[10] (Cost indices do not include sales taxes on the vehicle.) Dramatic increases in production costs occur at the stage of integration of engine and driveline components (particularly in Argentina). Sheet metal for vehicle bodies also involves substantial cost increases. Column 13 in Table 4 indicates the magnitude of investment in equipment for manufacture of components and parts at progressive phases of domestic content. The "power train" (engine and transmission), makes up about 20 percent of vehicle value and represents the higher range of investment costs.

63.   Assembly of complete knocked down (c.k.d.) sets involves only moderate cost increases (Table 4, line 1). In fact, beyond a certain minimum scale,

---

[8] The policy of the Mexican Government is to keep prices on consumer goods down as a deflationary measure. They do this in automotive products through price controls, rigorous control of profit margins by end producer and through tax and import duty exemptions on materials and other production inputs including capital equipment.

[9] Domestic content value is derived from local prices as a percent of total vehicle cost, which give indices of value (columns 4, 8, and 12, weighted according to share of total content in columns 2, 6, and 8). Thus, high cost or highly protected components in the various stages contribute to overstating local content shares in terms of international (*c.i.f.*) prices.

[10] The "deletion allowance" is the amount deducted from the price of a completely knocked-down (c.k.d.) kit for the parts no longer imported because they are to be reproduced domestically. For example, for a complete kit priced at \$2,000, if 40 percent value normally priced at \$800 were deleted only \$500 might be credited as a deletion allowance. Thus, the residual price of a 60 percent kit would be \$1,500 (in place of the \$1,200 one would normally expect). Deletion allowance amounts are often based on marginal production costs, which are well below average *total* costs, including profit.

decentralization of assembly plants close to consumer markets is often economically advantageous. But it must be realized that with the production runs required by even the largest firms now located in developing countries, vehicles assembled overseas from c.k.d. units are more costly (3 to 10 percent more) than completely built up units from the exporting country. There are 30 to 40 percent savings on shipping costs because of the smaller freight volume, but these savings are offset by added costs of rust proofing and packaging against damage in shipping. Assembly and painting generally cost slightly more overseas than allowed as a deletion factor by the manufacturer. Even for low-volume producers in Sweden, special handling and packaging costs more than offset slight savings in assembly costs. Firms like Fiat have specialized in c.k.d. operations and have managed to reduce extra costs to a minimum.

64.    Tires, batteries, engine fluids, and flat glass are included under mandatory items (in Table 4, line 2). These are items generally manufactured locally for the parts replacement market even before domestic manufacture of new vehicles is undertaken. Items such as shock absorbers and small stampings (line 3) can be supplied with minimal additional investment in production capacity and are often produced by an established supplier manufacturing a similar item for refrigerators or other consumer goods. The forging or casting and machining of engine, axle or transmission parts (lines 4 and 5) involve both substantial investment and manufacturing know-how. In the USA there generally is only a narrow difference between supplier costs and what it would cost the manufacturer to make the item himself. In developing countries, in-plant costs, especially at competitive scale, tend to be much lower than supplier prices—the joint result of protectionist profits and technical inefficiency.[11] In large-scale, competitive economies with well-developed supplier capabilities, specialization among parts manufacturers is both feasible and advantageous (para. 52). The risk and uncertainty of markets and production in developing economies inhibit investment in parts manufacturing plants, especially when they are already manufactured locally, even if at a somewhat higher cost. It is generally necessary to persuade parts manufacturers in the home country (often with long-term contract assurances) to establish a manufacturing affiliate in the developing country, particularly in such items as wheel drums, brakes, and axles (line 7), areas in which domestic suppliers generally lack the required capital or technical capacity. The provision of sheet metal for vehicle

---

[11] Volvo's success in manufacturing a relatively low volume of passenger cars for the domestic and world markets is in large part attributable to corporate capabilities in designing and engineering automotive parts whose production is then subcontracted to domestic and other suppliers on very narrow margins of profit. Volvo has followed this pattern for over 40 years.

bodies (line 8) involves the heaviest investment commitments by manufacturers.

65. There are some interesting contrasts among Latin American producers. Certain international manufacturers consider Brazil the best source area for the price and quality of purchased materials and parts. The "closed-border" rule in Mexico, under which a manufacturer is forced to purchase from a local supplier once he is licensed and established, undermines the competitiveness of procurement. Brazil's costs are lower than Argentina's because: (a) the domestic market is larger; (b) manufacturers have been operating longer and have in many cases already written off capital costs for equipment that is still in good working order; and (c) Brazilian automobile manufacturers have had a longer period to develop suppliers, improve quality, and reduce costs. Price controls in Brazil and Mexico have also been an important factor in keeping down suppliers' profits and end-product costs. In Argentina, the trend has been toward great proliferation of vehicle models and parts manufacturers. This contrasts with Mexican attempts to "rationalize" production by limiting the number of vehicle models and standardizing components and parts production.

66. Chart 3 and Table 5 show that the major element contributing to the high costs of vehicle manufacture in Latin America is local procurement of materials and parts, which are either protected or carry high import duties. In Argentina, material and parts average 3.3 times US cost levels, and they constitute about 75 percent of total costs. Administrative and selling costs (4 to 7 percent of total costs) are twice as high in Mexico as in the USA, and six times as high in Argentina. Interest charges (and exchange depreciation losses) average about $126 per vehicle in Brazil as compared to under $2 in the United States. Special tooling amortization is also nearly three times as expensive per vehicle in Brazil and Mexico (on considerably smaller production volumes) as in the United States.

67. Capital costs per unit manufactured increase considerably at lower volumes of production. A European firm reported the following investment costs for production of a small passenger car in Europe:

*Indices 180,000 production p.a. = 100*

| Annual Production (Units) | Investment (US$ millions) | Production | Investment | Investment Cost per Unit |
|---|---|---|---|---|
| 180,000 | $125 | 100 | 100 | 100 |
| 60,000 | 75 | 33 | 60 | 182 |
| 3,000 | 25 | 2 | 20 | 1,000 |

39

DAVIDSON COLLEGE LIBRARY
DAVIDSON, N. C.

TABLE 5: Cost Elements in the Manufacture of a Light Truck, USA, Argentina, Brazil and Mexico, January 1967

| | Dollar Costs[a] | | | | Percentages | | | | Ratios to US Costs | | |
|---|---|---|---|---|---|---|---|---|---|---|---|
| | USA | Argentina | Brazil | Mexico | USA | Argentina | Brazil | Mexico | Argentina | Brazil | Mexico |
| 1. Direct labor | 170.98 | 56.96 | 35.95 | 94.68 | 10.3 | 1.4 | 1.2 | 3.6 | 0.33 | 0.21 | 0.55 |
| 2. Material—local | 770.24 | 2,534.99 | 2,022.30 | 1,115.12 | 46.4 | 62.3 | 67.5 | 42.4 | 3.29 | 2.63 | 1.45 |
|       —import | — | 448.28 | 128.82 | 849.49 | — | 12.0 | 4.3 | 32.3 | — | — | — |
| 3. Variable manufacturing—overhead[c] | 335.32 | 224.14 | — | 71.01 | 20.2 | 6.0 | — | 2.7 | 0.73 | — | 0.21 |
| 4. Subtotal—variable cost | 1,276.54 | 3,324.37 | 2,187.07 | 2,130.30 | 76.9 | 81.7 | 73.0 | 81.0 | 2.60 | 1.71 | 1.67 |
| 5. Manufacturing—overhead[d] | 318.72 | 317.38 | 440.41 | 347.16 | 19.2 | 7.8 | 14.7 | 13.2 | 1.00 | 1.88 | 1.09 |
| 6. Special tooling amortization | 16.60 | 28.48 | 44.94 | 47.34 | 1.0 | 0.7 | 1.5 | 1.8 | 1.72 | 2.71 | 2.85 |
| 7. Administration and selling | 46.48 | 284.83 | 197.74 | 105.20 | 2.8 | 7.0 | 6.6 | 4.0 | 6.13 | 4.25 | 2.26 |
| 8. Subtotal—fixed cost | 381.80 | 630.69 | 638.09 | 449.70 | 23.0 | 15.5 | 22.8 | 19.0 | 1.65 | 1.79 | 1.31 |
| 9. Interest and other income expenses[e] | 1.66 | 113.94 | 125.84 | — | 0.1 | 2.8 | 4.2 | — | 68.64 | 75.81 | — |
| 10. Totals and averages[f] | 1,660.00[b] | 4,069.00 | 2,996.00 | 2,630.00 | 100.0 | 100.0 | 100.0 | 100.0 | 2.45 | 1.80 | 1.58 |

[a] Dollar costs for Latin countries converted at prevailing official exchange rate.
[b] The US vehicle is given an average cost ($1,660) for the three slightly different models at f.o.b. USA prices of $1,752 (Brazil), $1,604 (Mexico) and $1,634 (Argentina). See Table 3, column 6.
[c] Includes indirect labor, operating supplies, expendable tools, power, maintenance supplies, and scrap.

[d] Includes heating, some maintenance supplies, and some indirect labor.
[e] Includes losses due to exchange depreciation.
[f] Ratios shown here differ slightly from those given in Table 2 because the US base vehicle is not the same. See footnote b above.

*Source:* Calculated from data furnished by an American vehicle manufacturer.

CHART 3
COMPARISON OF COST ELEMENTS IN MANUFACTURE OF LIGHT TRUCKS
U.S., ARGENTINA, BRAZIL AND MEXICO, JANUARY 1967

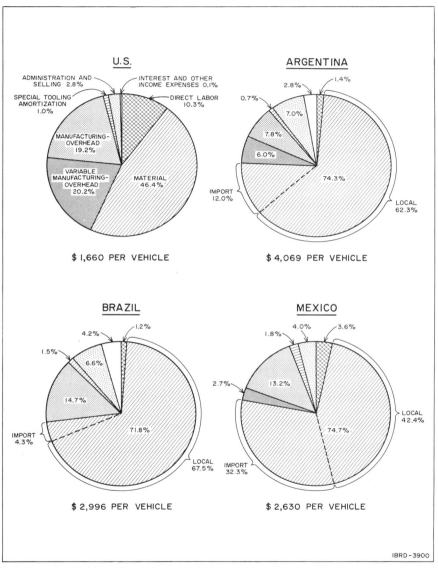

*Source:* See Table 5.

In most cases, firms have managed to keep capital charges down on short production runs by amortizing tooling dies on major vehicle components and body elements over a 5 to 10 year period. This is less of a problem on designs with longer life cycles than it is on the more rapidly changing US models. In order to minimize capital costs, Volkswagen in Brazil is continuing to manufacture the older body with smaller windows. Similarly, Volkswagen in Mexico retained the 1963 design until 1968. This is a small price to pay for the capital savings. Variations in capacity utilization of plant make a relatively slight difference to total costs because of the small percentage that are fixed costs. This is even more true of firms with a high percentage of outside procurement; their percentage of equipment and fixed costs are proportionately lower and their variable material costs higher.

# VI

# THE AUTOMOTIVE INDUSTRY
# IN ARGENTINA

68.  The Argentine industry has developed largely in the past decade under a regime of protection and progressive import substitution. Approximately 200,000 vehicles are now manufactured annually for the Argentine market. Prior to devaluation (1967), production costs were running at about 2.5 times a comparable duty-free import from an American or European plant. The basic reason for high costs is production at about one-tenth the scale of most European plants for an effective demand about one-sixth that of Italy. The proliferation of plants, further compounded by the wide range of models and makes, throws a heavy burden upon supplier industries.

## DEVELOPMENT OF THE DOMESTIC INDUSTRY

69.  Before 1955, 75 percent of the motor vehicles consumed in Argentina were imported with foreign exchange earned from agricultural exports. Subsequently balance-of-payments difficulties restricted imports of commercial vehicles and passenger cars. Under the Perón regime, the import of motor vehicles was a licensed privilege. The provisional government that followed Perón allowed the public to import cars subject to moderate surcharges, but the Frondizi Government sharply increased duties and encouraged the development of a domestic industry. National production was given its major impetus

by the Automotive Decree of March 1959. Under the provisions of this decree, domestic production has expanded nearly six times to the point where it now supplies 99 percent of Argentine demands. The decree also provided for progressive increases in national content (80 percent for trucks and 93 percent for passenger cars by the end of 1965).[1]

**TABLE 6:  Argentina, Imports, Consumption and Production, 1956–66**

| Year | Imported Vehicles & Chassis[a] | Total Consumption | Passenger Cars Produced[b] | Commercial Vehicles Produced[c] | Total Production | Percent Rise in Production |
|---|---|---|---|---|---|---|
| 1956 | 17,743 | 23,686 | 2,715 | 3,228 | 5,943 | – |
| 1957 | 47,187 | 62,822 | 11,743 | 3,892 | 15,635 | 163.1 |
| 1958 | 19,495 | 47,329 | 21,531 | 6,303 | 27,834 | 78.0 |
| 1959 | 6,915 | 39,745 | 23,816 | 9,014 | 32,830 | 17.9 |
| 1960 | 5,107 | 94,373 | 45,172 | 43,988 | 89,160 | 171.6 |
| 1961 | 4,947 | 141,213 | 81,932 | 54,334 | 136,266 | 52.8 |
| 1962 | 6,032 | 135,762 | 92,257 | 37,473 | 129,730 | − 4.8 |
| 1963 | 1,686 | 106,841 | 77,167 | 27,988 | 105,155 | −18.9 |
| 1964 | 1,286 | 167,769 | 115,855 | 50,628 | 166,483 | 58.3 |
| 1965 | 1,107 | 195,572 | 135,000 | 60,000 | 194,465 | 16.8 |
| 1966 | 1,461 | 180,914 | 123,937 | 55,516 | 179,453 | −7.7 |

[a] Includes assembled vehicles, chassis, accessories and replacement parts.
[b] Includes station wagons and jeeps.
[c] Includes pickups, delivery and other type trucks and chassis.
*Source:* Asociación de Fabricantes Argentinas (ADEFA); Consejo Nacional de Desarrollo (CONADE).

70.  Mercedes-Benz was the first major foreign firm to establish manufacturing operations in Argentina, in 1952. Their production plan provided for the development of domestic suppliers of components and parts and the progressive increase of domestic content. Industrias Kaiser Argentina (IKA) began operations in 1955. They purchased used equipment from the Kaiser plant in the United States including their own forging facilities. In 1963, they built their own axle and transmission plants and began supplying these parts to other manufacturers as well. By acquiring their own production facilities, they were assured a continued supply of quality parts in these critical items. Following the 1959 decree, Fiat, Ford, General Motors, Chrysler, and seven smaller firms entered the field. In 1965, Siam di Tella was purchased by Kaiser, and Chrysler purchased DKW. In July, 1967, Renault acquired the largest inter-

---

[1] Decree No. 3693, issued by the Ministry of Industry and Mining, later revised in August 1961 (Decree No. 6567) with subsequent amendments consolidated in the May 1965 Decree No. 3642. These percentage targets were later adjusted; by the end of 1966, domestic content ran about 92 percent for passenger vehicles and 86 percent on trucks (see Table 3).

est in IKA from Kaiser, assuming managerial control, and Ford purchased Transax, IKA's axle manufacturing subsidiary.

## GROWTH IN DOMESTIC DEMAND

71. The demand for automotive products in Argentina has been increasing well in advance of the growth of population and income in the past decade. Ownership density increased from one vehicle for every 32 inhabitants in 1955 to one for every 14 in 1965:

|  | 1955 | 1965 | Average Annual Growth Rate |
|---|---|---|---|
| Argentine population | 19,100,000 | 22,400,000 | 1.5% |
| Registered vehicles | 602,000 | 1,542,000 | 9.9% |
| Vehicle density (inhabitants per vehicle) | 32 | 14 | 8.2% |

Source: Asociación de Fábricas de Automotores, Report No. 267.

Intensified demand for automotive products more than doubled the car population in the ten-year period between 1955–1965. The decline in automotive prices since 1960 measured in constant pesos also contributed to rising demand.[2] Credit terms were also eased during this period; minimum cash-down payments were lowered and the length of the repayment period was extended. But in early 1966 the Government reversed the trend and increased excise taxes on passenger cars, in order to reduce foreign exchange deficits and release industrial resources to other sectors.

72. In the six-year period 1959–65, there was a sixfold increase in the output of passenger cars and trucks, from about 33,000 in 1959 to 195,000 in 1965. Argentina had an average annual rate of growth in automotive output of 35 percent, among the highest in the world in the past decade (Annex Table 7). Measured in terms of value added, the rate of growth during this period was even higher—tenfold or an average annual rate of 47 percent. Employment during this same period rose only threefold—increases in the scale of

---

[2] The wholesale price index rose 140 percent between 1960 and 1964, as compared to the automobile price index which increased by only 72 percent. This means that the relative price of vehicles at the end of 1964 measured at constant value was 28 percent below the 1960 level. The decline may be largely explained by intensified competition among the 13 manufacturers that eventually entered the market. (See ADEFA, *Informe Estadística*, No. 163, April 28, 1965.)

45

production leading to some productivity gains. The average annual rate of investment in 1960–64 was nearly ten times what it had been in 1956–59:

|  | 1956 | 1959 | 1965 |
|---|---|---|---|
| Vehicles assembled or manufactured | 5,900 | 32,800 | 195,000 |
| Employment | 3,700 | 11,600 | 34,600 |
| Value added (*million US$*) | .. | 46 | 465 |

|  | 1956–59 | 1960–64 |
|---|---|---|
| Average annual investment | 5.5 | 54.1 |
| (*million US$*) | | |

*Average annual growth rates, percent*

|  | 1956–59 | 1959–65 | 1956–65 |
|---|---|---|---|
| Vehicles | 75 | 35 | 46 |
| Employment | 46 | 17 | 28 |
| Value added | .. | 47 | .. |
| Investment | | | 33 (1956–64) |

*Source:* Consejo Nacional de Desarrollo, Argentina.

## PRESENT STRUCTURE OF THE INDUSTRY

73.    The Argentine automotive industry operates under severe diseconomies of scale. In 1965, Argentine production amounted to less than 2 percent of US output (Annex Table 16). There were thirteen manufacturers producing over 68 models of cars and trucks.[3] The six major manufacturers each turned out between 13,000 and 57,000 units; seven others produced between 500 and 6,600 each (Annex Table 12). There are several thousand component and parts manufacturers in Argentina, many operating out of small garage shops as sub-contractors to larger parts manufacturers. Chrysler alone reported 1500 supplier-vendors in 1965; about one-third of these were dual supplier sources.

74.    Intensified competition has led to a proliferation of makes and styles and frequent model changeovers; IKA's line advanced from 4 models in 1956 to 22 in 1963. Little or no effort has been made to standardize vehicle elements on bodies, chassis, engines, transmissions, electrical equipment, or brake and clutch systems—all of which compounded the basic difficulties of small-scale

---

[3] Aside from basic differences among passenger cars, trucks and buses, and a variety of other commercial-type vehicles, there are the differences in types of engines (horsepower, cylinders, gas/diesel, etc.), cooling systems, gear systems, electrical systems, wheel and tire sizes, chassis-types, various body sizes and shapes (and number of doors), spring suspension systems, axle widths, brake systems, etc.

production. Each manufacturer has also insisted upon developing his own suppliers, so that there are often as many as half a dozen suppliers even for such parts as radiators and batteries. Model proliferation adds to plant tooling costs and increases the burden of technical assistance on parts suppliers (see paras. 122–124).

75. Production volumes in Argentina are low by world standards, which means that Argentine plants can only afford equipment that must be used for a variety of purposes in order to minimize capital costs per unit of output. This results in considerable downtime on equipment. For example, heavy body dies for presses have to be changed for the several successive short runs of the 20 to 30 body panels in each passenger car or truck model. Low-volume equipment (single station, multi-purpose less-automated equipment) is used wherever possible for the manufacture of components and parts. For example, portable welding equipment and riveting guns are used for body assembly, rather than the heavier automatic equipment used by assembly plants in Detroit. Almost always this means higher unit costs for capital equipment than for plants elsewhere in the world employing mass production techniques. Below-capacity plant utilization is in part due to the economic recessions that have plagued the Argentine economy.[4] During periods of downturn, automotive firms are forced to carry underemployed labor and idle plant capacity, and this inevitably raises long-term average unit costs. Firms estimate that utilization varies between 20 and 60 percent in "bad" years and 70 to 80 percent in "good" years.[5]

76. The production cutbacks ordered in early 1966 further undermined efficient plant utilization. Production dropped from 195,000 units in 1965 to 160,000 units in 1966. These cutbacks were made in response to Argentina's

---

[4] Economic downturns tend to occur more frequently (about every 3 years) and with greater intensity (5.5 percent decrease in 1963 as compared with 8.6 percent growth in 1964) than they do in some more advanced industrial economies. Physical output of automotive vehicles has varied from a 172 percent increase during the 1959–60 boom period to a 19 percent decline in 1962–63 (Table 6).

[5] See Table 6 and Annex Table 14. Production at the Kaiser plant slumped from a peak of 170 vehicles a day in 1960–61 to 81 a day in 1963, then jumped back to 200 a day in 1964. Such variations are bound to increase average production costs. Utilization estimates depend upon whether equipment is normally used on a one-shift or multi-shift basis. Kaiser and, to a lesser degree, Fiat have equipped their plants for three-shift operations (Annex Table 13). At the Ford Plant, which was equipped largely for a one-shift operation, utilization of installed capacity rose from 16.8 percent for trucks and 23.7 percent for cars during the 1963 depression to 74.4 percent and 78.2 percent respectively in 1965. The fixed assets to value added ratio fell from 5.4 in 1963 to 2.8 in 1964; and there were 3.4 employees per 100,000 pesos of value added in 1963 as compared to only 1.5 in 1964.

deteriorating balance-of-payments difficulties toward the end of 1965, but the economy had to pay the additional price of reduced production efficiency. At least two years' lead time is needed to prepare a realistic production plan for adjusting to such changes in production quotas or for integrating new components under a revised domestic-content regulation. (For reference to a similar situation in New Zealand, see para. 112.) Industry was told in May, 1965, to plan on cutbacks in January, 1966, but no one realized how severe they would be. Considerable time and resources were spent in complying with Government regulations and report requirements—as much as twelve man-years per year reported by one firm. The turnover in Government personnel issuing administrative orders further compounded the problems. Perhaps one result was the inflexibility on the part of the industrialization authorities in allowing individual manufacturers to adjust to different sets of circumstances. For example, when Bendix Brakes went out of business in 1963, Chrysler was fined heavily because it was forced to import brakes.

*Supplier Problems*

77. Automotive manufacturers experience great difficulty in obtaining an adequate supply of required components and parts. Quality has been deficient on such items as electrical equipment (spark plugs, starters, ignition coils, distributors, and various instruments). Difficulty has also been experienced with forgings and castings (especially aluminum castings and iron engine blocks), chrome-plated items (grill work and bumpers) and various plastics and vinyls (in some cases reverting to paper-covered wires proved more practical and cheaper). Most body manufacturers have had to import sheet steel of the type produced in Argentina, because the local product had substandard ductility when used in the heavy-duty stamping presses, and consequently a high rejection rate.

*Manpower Situation*

78. Except for periodic shortages of craftsmen (e.g. tool-die makers and skilled machinists), the recruitment and training of industrial labor has posed no major obstacle. Workers are considered (by international managers) very skillful with their hands and there is a good supply of technical people. There has been a turnover problem with the rise and fall of economic activity. Many of the technicians trained by the automotive industry are lost when work falls off; others have left in good times to set up their own garage operations to produce components or parts for the industry. (There is a strong inclination among Argentinians to own their own business, regardless of the opportunity cost.)

*Comparative Costs and Balance-of-Payments Effects*

79.   The analysis of Argentine costs appears in Chapter V. It shows that in January 1967 a light truck which could be produced for $1,634 in the United States, cost about $4,069 to manufacture in Argentina or 2.5 times as much (Table 3). The basic contribution to high cost was the procurement of materials and parts that are produced in very short runs or have a high markup due to protection. Procurement costs averaged 3.3 times as much in Argentina as in the USA. Understandably, price differences are larger on components and parts that are typically high-volume in the United States; generally speaking, the cost gap is proportional to the production volume gap. The cost differential is especially high on a part such as a crankshaft, which has a good amount of intricate milling. It is produced largely by automatic equipment in the United States, but by hand-machining in Argentina for the low volumes demanded. Other high-cost items include pistons, starters, and clutches (Annex Table 15).

80.   The above figures on comparative costs are corroborated by another set of data obtained during the field mission to Argentina. These showed that ex-factory prices of cars and trucks in Argentina averaged about 2.5 times those in the United States (Annex Table 16). Kaiser reported a difference of 1.8 times on the jeep, which sold for $3,188 in Argentina as compared to $1,728 in the United States. But on its higher-priced passenger car, the delivered price was 2.9 times its US counterpart. At export prices which allow special drawbacks and a more favorable exchange rate, IKA was able to deliver a jeep to an adjacent Latin American market for $1,707, or slightly under the *f.o.b.* US list price.[6]

81.   A major consideration in mounting the import substitution program was to conserve foreign exchange. The rationale behind the Automotive Decree of 1959 was that substantial increases in domestic consumption of automotive vehicles would be realized without appreciable increases in foreign exchange expenditures. But the mounting foreign exchange burden forced the production cutbacks of 1966. The Government hoped to expand production from about 32,800 vehicles in 1959 to about 200,000 in 1965 without increasing the foreign exchange burden much beyond the 1959 level (then estimated at $26

---

[6] This is at an exchange rate of 225 pesos to the dollar in December 1965, which would have corrected for overvaluation as reflected in the rise of domestic prices since 1958/59. At the official rate of 179 pesos to the dollar, the export price was $2,146 (Annex Table 17). It should also be borne in mind that Argentine vehicle models are somewhat different from similar models in the United States. For example, among other differences, 1965 Ford (Argentina) trucks have 1964 bodies and 1959 engines.

million). Table 7 shows how the actual burden rose from about $42 million in 1959 to about $126 million in 1965 (including some $40 to $50 million for remittances of earnings).

**TABLE 7: Foreign Exchange Cost, Argentina, 1959 and 1965**

| | 1959 | 1965 |
|---|---|---|
| 1. Vehicles produced in Argentina | 32,800 | 195,000 |
| 2. Total cost at $4,069[a] equivalent per vehicle | $133 million | $793 million |
| 3. Cost of comparable imports at $2,300[b] c.i.f. | $ 75 million | $449 million |
| 4. Planned import allowance | 34 percent[c] | 10 percent[d] |
| 5. Estimated foreign exchange cost (line 3 x line 4) | $ 26 million | $ 45 million |
| 6. Actual import allowances[e] | 56 percent[f] | 28 percent[g] |
| 7. Foreign exchange cost at $2,300 price level (line 3 x line 6) | $ 42 million | $126 million |
| 8. Foreign exchange cost at $4,069 price level[h] (line 2 x line 6) | $ 74 million | $222 million[i] |

[a] Average ex-factory price of a light truck, Table 3 (column 3), p. 38.

[b] Average c.i.f. price of a Kaiser vehicle, Annex Table 17.

[c] Weighted average of the 1959 allowable import content of 30 percent for cars (72.5 percent of product), and 45 percent for trucks (27.5 percent of product).

[d] March 1959 decree of the Ministry of Industry. Under subsequent revisions, import content in 1965 was 9 percent for cars and 28 percent for trucks.

[e] After allowing for the import content of locally procured components. For a Falcon costing $3,777 locally to produce in 1964, $1,831 represented locally procured components, of which one-third or $610 is estimated foreign content, or 16 percent of the cost of local production of a car. For a F-100 truck costing $3,179 locally, $1,293 were locally procured components, of which $431 or 14 percent of local costs were foreign content.

[f] The import content of cars in 1959 was 30 percent plus an estimated 33 percent of the 70 percent local content = 53 percent. The import content for trucks was 45 percent plus 33 percent of the 55 percent local content = 63 percent. Weighting as in note c gives 56 percent.

[g] The import content of cars in 1965 was 9 percent plus an estimated 15 percent of 91 percent = 23 percent. The import content of trucks was 28 percent plus an estimated 15 percent of the 72 percent = 39 percent. In 1965, 69 percent of production was in cars and 31 percent in trucks. This weighting gives 28 percent overall.

[h] Measuring imported resources at Argentine manufacturing costs.

[i] The Central Bank estimated the foreign exchange burden imposed on the Argentine economy by the automotive industry in 1965 at about $250 million. According to CONADE input-output estimates, the import coefficient for automobiles and tractors was .244 per dollar in 1960. (See Annex Table 19.) If the 1960 coefficient is applied to 1965 output of $793 million, the import content would be $194 million.

82. In the years immediately following the 1959 decree, firms were able to earn substantial profits on the allowed 40 percent import content on which the duty averaged 30 percent, as compared to over 150 percent on assembled vehicles. The decline of consumer prices (netting out the inflationary trend), coupled with costs rising as a function of domestic content, has probably resulted in a narrowing of profits for surviving firms. In 1964, which was a "good" year, profits after taxes ranged between about 5 and 10 percent of sales and about 20 to 30 percent on shareholders' equity (Annex Table 18). This appears favorable when compared with reported earnings by US automotive firms of 6 to 7 percent profits after tax on sales in 1964/65 and 16 to 21 percent on shareholders' equity.[7]

83. Reported earnings varied widely among firms, from a high of 13.7 percent after tax on sales reported by Fiat to a 2.5 percent loss reported by Mercedes Benz (Annex Table 18). Losses during bad years have been offset by tax write-offs, so that the net gains have been substantial. Fiat managed to do well from the outset; they were especially astute in negotiating their agreement with the Argentine Government and in earning substantial profits from high percentages of import content. Annex Table 14 also shows that they had a high labor productivity. During 1966, when most firms were forced to cut back production, Fiat managed to expand production by more than 30 percent, from about 26,000 to 34,000 units.

84. Kaiser probably did well until late 1965; they got an early start, developed essential parts production capability, and successfully diversified the vehicle line to meet competition without overtaxing production capabilities. IKA's production dropped from about 54,000 units by about one-third between November 1965 and November 1966. But, ironically, its demise in mid-1967 was in part due to an over-extension made possible by its leading position in the industry. In absorbing Siam di Tella in 1965, IKA hoped to gain an additional 5,000 vehicle production authorization along with forging and casting facilities in the Buenos Aires area (IKA was located largely in Cordoba).

---

[7] See Federal Trade Commission (SEC), *Quarterly Financial Report,* Fourth Quarter 1965. Reported profits and international comparisons should be taken with several grains of salt. To begin with, Argentine profits on equity are overstated due to under-evaluation of assets as a result of the 20 to 35 percent annual rate of inflation. Secondly, in addition to corporate profits of the Argentine corporation, the international firm also realizes income from the sale of components and parts and from licensing and technical assistance fees, which would probably double reported earnings of the US corporations from these overseas subsidiaries.

They bought into a firm with underestimated liabilities just before the cutbacks ordered by the Government in late 1965.

## CRITIQUE OF ARGENTINE EXPERIENCE

85.   The import substitution policies initiated by the Argentine government resulted in the rapid growth of an indigenous industry, but the price was high in terms of comparative costs of production and a mounting foreign exchange burden. The theory behind the industrialization program was that growth could be achieved within the constraint of foreign exchange shortages. Argentina planned for a sixfold expansion in the number of domestically manufactured vehicles between 1959–65 on the basis that there would be no appreciable increase in foreign exchange requirements. In fact, foreign exchange costs expanded nearly five times during this period. To this extent, the program of import substitution designed to save foreign exchange and increase output from available resources was self-defeating.

86.   Industrialization policies have resulted in a large number of vehicles and parts manufacturers that are inefficient by world standards. There are too many plants and too many models and makes for a market the size of Argentina. Argentine consumption followed the general pattern of demand in more affluent societies that can afford product differentiation because of higher income levels and more efficient industrial organization. However even in France and Germany, in the post-World War II period, Citroën and Volkswagen mass-produced small cars with no model changes in order to take advantage of scale factors (see para. 123). Protection and import controls associated with Argentina's industrialization policy raised the cost structure throughout the economy, distorted price mechanisms, and undermined future growth and expansion of industrial sectors. Commercially, the automotive industry suffered from a combination of erratic demand, adverse supply conditions, and periodic narrowing of profits in times of recession or cutback.

87.   Rapid development of local content has added to internal inflationary pressures as new demands on domestic resources for materials, skills, and capital equipment outstripped the economy's supply capabilities. Costs also rose as less expensive imported materials and parts were replaced by domestically manufactured goods. In the indiscriminate pursuit of autarky, engineering and managerial skills were spread too thin in too wide a range of components and parts manufactured for too many low-volume vehicle models. The system of import restrictions and a lagging exchange rate have distorted price mecha-

nisms and resulted in the misallocation of critical resources such as foreign exchange and capital equipment.

88. Intensified competition from too many producers in a limited market, coupled with the emphasis upon styling and model proliferation as the major device for a firm to maintain its market share, resulted in an inevitable cost-profit squeeze. This, added to increasing difficulties on remittances of earnings because of Argentina's balance-of-payments difficulties, eroded the overseas incentive to invest in Argentina. Most Argentine automotive firms have also experienced difficulties in adjusting to abrupt changes in production schedules brought on by chronic balance-of-payments difficulties.

89. The high cost structure induced by protection undermined Argentina's future chances for entering and competing in larger regional or world markets, which are the major opportunities for future growth and more efficient production at larger scales. The prospects for regional development are still poor (see paras. 125–131). To enter world markets, plants must be internationally cost competitive and must maintain international quality and reliability standards. The system of protection also created vested interests representing inefficient managements and plants. A lagging exchange rate, which in effect subsidized import substitution industries, is not compatible with industrialization strategies dependent upon export activities (see para. 137).

# VII

## CURRENT DEVELOPMENTS
## IN YUGOSLAVIA

90.   Yugoslavia is an interesting and important case study in the development of the automotive industry. The Yugoslav system of economic planning enabled them to control consumption patterns in terms of product range and quantities. They have also managed foreign exchange costs more effectively than the Argentines. But there has been an overproliferation of plants and suppliers in truck manufacture, and nonstandardized models and parts have contributed to high costs. Foreign exchange shortages have forced domestic production of parts that are costly to produce in short series or expensive to stockpile. The Yugoslavs felt the need to liberalize their international trading in 1965 in order to eliminate their own high cost production. Exporting to soft currency areas has been one means for increasing production volume. Yugoslavia is also an interesting case as a country in the intermediate stage of industrial development that has now become a transmitter of technology to countries like Egypt and Indonesia partly through barter trade arangements and partly due to the fact that their product designs and production techniques approximate the income and scale requirements of these countries.

### ECONOMIC POLICIES

91.   The Yugoslavs have been highly pragmatic in their drive toward economic efficiency under "market socialism." They realize that the next major

54

step in economic development is to find ways and means to increase production volumes. There is just so much that can be done internally and no more. They have standardized parts, integrated plants, and increased complementary production among trading partners under barter arrangements. The Economic Reform of 1965—in effect a series of economic reforms[1]—is designed to liberalize controls over the management of Yugoslav firms and enable them to become part of the international division of labor. Under the reform, Yugoslav firms were given wide latitude in utilizing dinar profits and exchange earnings for reinvestment and future growth. This not only puts production units on a more economic basis, it also exposes industrial sectors to international pricing and leads to a more efficient use of national resources. The Yugoslavs realize that competition in world markets is intensifying, and the sooner Yugoslavia exposes its economy to competitive forces the better. Under the 1965 reforms, independent decision-making was authorized at the enterprise level in the fields of marketing, production, and investment—a major departure from the system of centralized planning that prevailed in the 1950's. Enterprises are free to choose suppliers, set prices on their products, and decide how to use profits for investments in future growth. The criterion of enterprise decision is income maximization "within the framework of social objectives." The regulations provide for autonomy in negotiating cooperation with foreign partners including agreements on production specialization. Thus enterprises plan their foreign trade with a view to maximizing revenue and obtaining the best sources of supply.

## MARKET STRUCTURE AND COMPARATIVE COSTS

92.　In 1965, about 36,000 passenger cars and 12,000 trucks and buses were being manufactured and assembled in Yugoslavia. One firm produced all the passenger cars and nine manufactured trucks. The major passenger car and truck manufacturers have been exploring ways and means to rationalize domestic production and enter into broader international arrangements to specialize and trade in components and assembled vehicles. But Yugoslav firms are inhibited in their efforts by capital and foreign exchange shortages and have been seeking ways to broaden relationships with foreign partners in order to more effectively absorb foreign techniques, enlarge market access, and expand the scale of production. The problem of entering into international arrangements that are compatible with the legal framework of socialist ownership has been largely resolved.

---

[1] See Federal Institute of Economic Planning (Yugoslavia), *Planning of Foreign Trade—the Yugoslav Experience* (Belgrade: FIEP, March 1967), pp. 10–15.

93. Cost comparisons are somewhat deceptive in that they do not reflect relative efficiencies in terms of resource requirements at international prices. Under the exchange and tariff structures that prevail in Yugoslavia,[2] the export price of a locally manufactured Fiat 600 is $1,000, which is just below the ex-factory price in Italy, $1024. (See below.) Production volume in Yugoslavia is about 1/25 that of Fiat in Italy. Prices to Yugoslav consumers are considerably above the export price.

## PRODUCTION STRATEGIES FOR YUGOSLAV PLANTS

94. Zavodi Crvena Zastava, the largest passenger car plant in Yugoslavia, operates under a Fiat license. It manufactured and assembled over 40,000 vehicles in 1966. Dealerships have been established in Greece, where Yugoslav "Fiats" are sold in competition with Italian Fiats. Substantial amounts of Fiat replacement parts are also marketed in Greece. CZ dealers compete there with Italian Fiat dealers by selling at a lower markup and providing wider choices to customers on accessories and trim. Fiat tolerates Yugoslav competition in Greece because of its long-term interest in Yugoslavia as a gateway to Eastern European markets.

95. CZ is intensifying its efforts to reduce production costs by (a) maximizing the use of existing capacity, and (b) increasing parts series volume through specialization and interchange among Fiat affiliates in other Eastern European countries. But the major opportunities for future growth now lie in external markets.

96. Under an agreement with Fiat signed early in 1968, production at the CZ plant, 35,000 units in 1965, is to be increased to 75,000 by 1969 and 130,000 by 1972. Fiat has invested $10 million and has a 10 percent share in the joint venture. Fiat has also agreed to upgrade the technical capabilities of its Yugoslav partner, including the establishment of a Zastava office in Torino, Italy. The Italian partner has also agreed to absorb into its international marketing and manufacturing system an average annual $5 million in Yugoslav vehicles and parts over the next ten years. This extended agreement would permit Yugoslavia to make the critical jump from production limited to domestic consumption to a more efficient higher volume for regional and world markets. The magnitude of the proposed change is large enough to move Yugoslavia's automotive industry to the next development plateau.

---

[2] The dinar was devalued in 1965 from 750 to 1,250 dinars to the US dollar, and tariffs on imports were adjusted downward so as not to increase supplier costs.

It would also substantially improve economic efficiency in the automotive sector in terms of resource utilization and balance-of-payments effect. Under such an arrangement, Yugoslavia will earn sufficient foreign exchange to pay for an expanded foreign content in other models assembled locally, and thereby eliminate domestic procurement on items that are high-cost or otherwise unsatisfactory.

97.   The largest commercial vehicle manufacturer in Yugoslavia is Tovorna Autombilov in Motorjev (TAM). It manufactured approximately 3,400 two- to five-ton trucks and 400 buses in 1965 under a German license—about a third of national output. Some 13 percent of TAM's output, or US $4.5 million in vehicles and parts, was exported. This more than paid for the $3.5 million in import requirements. For a broad view of Yugoslavia's balance of automotive trade, the reader should turn to Annex Table 20.

98.   The TAM factory has proposed expanding production from 3,900 trucks and buses in 1965 to 5,200 in 1968, essentially to make use of installed equipment which was underutilized. It hopes to improve production efficiency in the following additional ways: (a) widen cooperation among vehicle producers in Yugoslavia and in neighboring countries by specialization and interchange, (b) standardize truck models and parts where possible, (c) consolidate parts suppliers and weed out marginal producers in Yugoslavia, (d) persuade German licensors to take Yugoslav parts in exchange for required German imports,[3] and (e) consolidate their holdings with developing countries such as Indonesia which has licensing arrangements with TAM.

99.   The rationalization program outlined above may be quite sound as a limited adjustment program. But it does not resolve the larger issue of long-term economic viability. Production is still low volume by international standards and the diseconomies of small-scale are compounded by near-100 percent domestic content. Even if all the truck manufacturers in Yugoslavia were combined, their scale of operation would be small by European standards. The total Yugoslav truck market in 1965 was about 10,000. Several European firms manufacturing under 15,000 trucks a year are now running into the problem of survival.

---

[3] TAM must deliver about 20 percent below German supplier prices in order to absorb a 16 percent German tariff and 5 percent additional freight cost. At one time, TAM's exports to Germany reached US$2.5 million, but they are now down to about $0.5 million.

100. A basic problem in the industrial equipment field is keeping up with major innovations in product designs. Another problem relates to industrial design. Yugoslav industrialists have expressed an understandable desire to develop their own engineering and design capabilities. They realize they must do this eventually if they are to compete in international markets. But the difficulty is that it takes considerable capital and human resources to develop new products and to establish international marketing networks. The co-production and co-marketing arrangements with European vehicle and parts manufacturers represent a transitional stage which could lead to financial and technical assistance in implanting design and marketing capabilities.[4]

---

[4] See paras. 144–146.

# VIII

## AUTOMOTIVE INDUSTRY IN
## NEW ZEALAND

101.   New Zealand has a per capita income higher than all European countries except Sweden. This is largely due to a very efficient wool and dairy industry, which earns nearly one-fourth of the national income through exports to world markets. But the industrial sector is another matter. It has been protected for nearly 30 years, and manufactured goods produced domestically cost between 50 and 100 percent more than comparable duty-free imports. Progressive autarky has been adopted as the basic strategy to provide growth and employment, and relative costs have been virtually disregarded. New Zealand, like many newly industrializing countries, is now confronted with the problem of continued growth in the face of mounting balance-of-payments deficits. The automotive sector in New Zealand is following a course of development similar to that of Argentina under an analagous regime of protection and import substitution. Ten firms are now producing for a market of only 70,000 vehicles. At 40 percent domestic content, costs per vehicle are already running 60 percent above the *c.i.f.* price—and the domestic value added is itself 135 percent more than the comparable international cost. The New Zealand experience helps to isolate the adverse effects of progressive autarky in small-scale markets —regardless of the overall stage of economic development.[1]

---

[1] See also para. 58 and Annex Table 11 where cost differences between India and the United Kingdom, at the same scales of production, are compared.

# ECONOMIC POLICIES

102. The demand for and supply of automotive products has been strongly influenced by government economic policies since 1950. A program of import substitution was instituted to overcome shortages in the supply of vehicles and to minimize foreign exchange costs. Measures to curtail consumption or restrict production in order to reduce foreign exchange expenditures have been reactivated periodically in response to recurrent balance-of-payments difficulties. The foreign exchange burden has risen, despite government efforts to increase domestic content (Table 8). By mid-1966, the foreign exchange burden generated by vehicle consumption rose to about NZ$47 million.[2]

103. Vehicles are manufactured in New Zealand under a system of protection and import control designed to save foreign exchange and encourage domestic manufacture of parts. The tariff schedule favors the import of vehicles in a knocked-down form (c.k.d. packs) and vehicles and parts of

**TABLE 8: Vehicle Imports into New Zealand, 1960–66**

| | | Complete Knocked-Down Units | | Other | | Total | |
|---|---|---|---|---|---|---|---|
| | | No. | c.i.f. value (NZ$[a] million) | No. | c.i.f. value (NZ$ million) | No. | c.i.f. value (NZ$ million) |
| *Passenger Cars* | 1960/61 | 32,804 | 10.3 | 2,576 | 1.5 | 35,380 | 11.8 |
| | 1962/63 | 38,003 | 14.3 | 4,006 | 2.6 | 42,009 | 16.9 |
| | 1963/64 | 61,680 | 22.7 | 7,150 | 4.8 | 68,830 | 27.5 |
| | 1964/65 | 56,775 | 21.4 | 8,570 | 5.5 | 65,345 | 26.9 |
| | 1965/66 | 58,718 | 22.0 | 8,035 | 5.2 | 66,753 | 27.2 |
| *Trucks* | 1960/61 | 10,870 | 5.0 | 694 | 0.4 | 11,564 | 5.4 |
| | 1962/63 | 8,075 | 4.1 | 180 | 0.1 | 8,255 | 4.2 |
| | 1963/64 | 8,859 | 4.7 | 97 | 0.3 | 8,956 | 5.0 |
| | 1964/65 | 9,505 | 5.5 | 131 | 0.2 | 9,636 | 5.7 |
| | 1965/66 | 13,134 | 9.1 | 117 | 0.3 | 13,251 | 9.4 |
| *Totals* | 1960/61 | 43,674 | 15.3 | 3,270 | 1.9 | 46,944 | 17.2 |
| | 1962/63 | 46,078 | 18.4 | 4,186 | 2.7 | 50,264 | 21.1 |
| | 1963/64 | 70,539 | 27.4 | 7,247 | 5.1 | 77,786 | 32.5 |
| | 1964/65 | 66,280 | 26.9 | 8,701 | 5.7 | 75,081 | 32.6 |
| | 1965/66 | 71,852 | 31.1 | 8,152 | 5.5 | 80,004 | 36.6 |

[a] NZ$1.00 = $1.40.
*Source:* New Zealand Department of Statistics.

[2] NZ$1.00 equaled US$1.40 before devaluation in November 1967. About NZ$37 million is reported as direct imports of c.k.d. packs and other vehicles (Table 8); at least another NZ$10 million should be added for import content of domestic parts and for overseas payment of royalties, licensing fees, and earnings on foreign equity or loans.

Commonwealth origin.[3] In practice, the system of import licensing and foreign exchange controls provides absolute protection from imported vehicles. The general policy has been to award each firm an exchange quota based upon the value of imports (and production volume) in previous years.[4] This limits the number of vehicles that can be manufactured and sold. (For an exception, see para. 109.)

104.   Prior to 1940, nearly two-thirds of the vehicles supplied to the New Zealand market were assembled locally; value added was largely labor and paint. During the 1950's, local industries began supplying tires, batteries, radiators and interior trim. Seat frames, springs, hubcaps, air filters and other interior trim items were added after 1962/63.

105.   Before 1961, it was believed that the grant of a *fixed* percentage of foreign exchange, based on production volume in the previous period, was sufficient incentive to increase domestic content, since the greater the use of domestic components, the less the exchange cost per vehicle, and the more vehicles or packs or parts a firm could sell. The percentage allotment proved insufficient, and a new bonus incentive scheme was introduced in 1961, which increased the percentage of foreign exchange allocated to firms according to increases in their domestic content:

| For domestic content that reached in value: | Increase in import license of: |
|---|---|
| 35.0% | 7.5% |
| 37.5% | 10.0% |
| 40.0% | 15.0% |
| 42.5% | 17.5% |
| 45.0% | 20.0% |

In practice, the scheme was unattractive to vehicle manufacturers beyond the 40 percent domestic content level, as it failed to take into account the substantial increases in production costs associated with further increases in domestic content. The low deletion allowances accorded by foreign manufacturers for excluded items added to the disincentive. (See para. 111.)

---

[3] The duty on c.k.d. packs was 6¼ percent *ad valorem* on Commonwealth origin and 45 percent from most-favored nations; on built-up vehicles the duties were 20 percent and 55 percent respectively.

[4] In 1963/64, when the Government was under pressure to increase the availability of motor cars, additional import authorizations were allocated on the basis of sales performance by car assembly plants in that year.

106. In March 1965, a revised motor vehicles manufacturing scheme was issued covering local assembly of c.k.d. packs in batches of 300 to 600 units. Account was taken of the overseas deletion allowance in preparing the list of parts required to be processed locally. The memorandum also stipulated that the price of these new products was not to exceed that of comparable imported built-up vehicles—an unrealistic stipulation in view of the increased cost of domestic production already experienced. The paperwork alone connected with licensing ten firms manufacturing nearly 50 models has been formidable. Manufacturing schemes had to be accompanied by full details of items deleted, deletion allowances by overseas suppliers, the cost of local product, and sources of local procurement. One particular bone of contention between the government and individual firms has been agreement over what in fact constitutes "factory costs"—a rather complicated piece of arithmetic difficult to define and even more difficult to administer.

107. By 1961, domestic content had reached an average of just over 30 percent. By mid-1963, under the 1961 bonus scheme, domestic content increased to an average of 40 percent. Some firms added items such as spark plugs, ignition coils, wiring systems, and shock absorbers. Under the March 1965 incentive scheme, the Government requested that the remaining vehicle manufacturers add these and other "hang-on" items such as driveshafts, wheels, and carburetors. Such items are much more complicated from a technical standpoint and involve substantial new investment for a relatively low volume of diversified parts. Domestic content reported by individual firms in 1967 ranged between a low of 32 percent and a high of 48 percent—an average of about 40 percent, the level already attained in 1963. In July 1967, in response to the worsening balance-of-payments position, the Ministry of Industry and Commerce issued a letter to the automotive industry calling for further increases of domestic content to 50 percent, since the automotive sector was one of the few areas where the Government had leverage to control exchange expenditures.

## COMPARATIVE COSTS OF PRODUCTION

108. Production costs in New Zealand are running approximately 60 percent above c.i.f. prices. A vehicle priced internationally at NZ$2,000 c.i.f. now costs NZ$3,200 to manufacture in New Zealand at 40 percent domestic content. It cost NZ$1,880 in domestic resources to produce NZ$800 worth of domestic content—or 2.35 times international cost.[5] The consumer pays

---

[5] Assuming 10 percent duty on the 60 percent imported content worth NZ$1,200, the import content costs $1,320; the domestic content therefore costs NZ$1,880. Total vehicle costs are made up as follows: .60 (1.10) + .40 (2.35) = 1.6 times the c.i.f. price.

considerably more than NZ$3,200, in some cases up to NZ$5,400 (NZ$800 tax plus as much as NZ$1,400 premium on a new car without a purchase authorization or trade-in).[6]

109. Diseconomy of small-scale production is a basic contribution to high costs. The entire industry in New Zealand assembled about 59,000 passenger cars and 13,000 trucks and other commercial vehicles in 1965–66 (estimated from c.k.d. imports in Table 8). Seven firms accounted for about 80 percent of vehicle assembly volume—an average of 8,000 vehicles per firm, which is quite low by international standards.[7] In all, there are at least 10 firms operating 17 plants turning out 40 to 50 different passenger car models (Annex Table 21). The proliferation of models and makes is aggravated by so-called "no remittance" purchases. Under present government regulations, purchasers with foreign exchange assets are not subject to rationing and may place an order for the assembly and delivery of any model or make. One-third of General Motors sales in 1966–67 were in this category.

110. At low production volumes, costs rise as a function of domestic content. This tendency is clear in other developing countries with national production volumes two and three times that of New Zealand. Judging by the Latin American experience, the New Zealand Government's announced policy urging vehicle manufacturers to increase domestic content from 40 to 50 percent could increase the average cost per vehicle to 80 percent above the *c.i.f.* price (Chart 2).[8] This cost increase estimate may be considered a minimum, since it is based on production runs of 20,000 to 30,000 in Latin America as compared to under 10,000 in New Zealand. (See Table 1.)

---

[6] See the next paragraph for "no remittance" purchase authorizations, which are worth up to 45 percent above the c.k.d. value.

[7] See Table 1 for international comparisons.

[8] In the 40 to 50 percent domestic content range, it is estimated costs will increase by a factor of 3.1 for 10 percentage points of local content—the combined result of increased costs for domestic manufacture and low deletion allowance (see next footnote, and footnote 9, para. 62). Thus for every NZ$1 of *c.i.f.* value, it has been estimated that manufacturing costs will increase by a factor of 2.1 over a deletion allowance of only NZ$0.68, or $\dfrac{2.10}{0.68} = 3.1$

(compare to lines 5 and 6, column 1 in Table 4, which show cost increase factors ranging from 1.9 to 4.0 for this range of local content in Argentina). The average cost increment in New Zealand (recalculating from data in footnote 5, para. 108) would then be .50(1.10) + .40(2.35) + .10(3.10) = 1.8.

111.   Most firms have found it unprofitable to manufacture cars with more than 40 percent domestic content. Increased costs of domestic production outweigh realizable profits resulting from additional import authorizations. This is because the allowance by overseas suppliers for deleted components and parts is usually well below the *c.i.f.* price. At the same time, the local cost of low-volume domestic manufacture is well above the *c.i.f.* price.[9] Moreover, at a time when profits are falling, firms are being asked to increase their investments in plant and equipment to manufacture vehicles and parts. This is especially true of production beyond 40 percent domestic content, which means manufacturing the more costly and sophisticated parts for engines, transmissions and other elements of the power train.

112.   In its efforts to deal with the balance-of-payments deficit, the government has not only urged the industry to increase domestic content, it has also tightened consumer credit on car purchases. Up to that time there had been a car shortage (estimated at 10 percent as measured by advanced orders for cars). After credit was tightened, the drop in the demand for passenger cars resulted in an estimated 30 percent surplus in new car stocks.[10] If implemented, the government order would cut back production from the current level of about 70,000 vehicles to about 56,000 units by mid-1969. Such drastic fluctuations in the level of effective demand play havoc on efficient plant operations. The combined effect of increased costs and the drop in revenue from car sales is bound to place automotive firms in a cost-profit squeeze. This approach to balance-of-payments difficulties results in a two-fold decrease in overall economic efficiency: resource costs for domestic content are increased, and installed plant capacity is underutilized.

113.   The alternative to further import substitution is specialization in selective components and parts for export to manufacturing affiliates in nearby countries. This would mean that the next 10 percent of value added would be

---

[9] One firm estimated it costs NZ$38 per vehicle to manufacture locally an additional five percent domestic content, for which they were given a deletion allowance of NZ$18 per vehicle. This meant an additional cost of NZ$20 per vehicle. The additional profit on the 10 percent mark-up on factory costs of NZ$1,150 (NZ$115) did not cover the increased cost on a 3,000 unit run. The 15 percent increase on import license meant an authorization for an additional 450 vehicles. Thus: 3,000 + 450 vehicles × $20 increased cost per vehicle ($69,000) is more than the added profits from 450 additional vehicles at $115 unit profit ($51,750).

[10] On hire-purchase sales, cash-down payment requirements were raised from 50 percent to 66⅔ percent and repayment period reduced from 18 to 12 months.

in the least-cost range, thereby lowering rather than increasing average total costs of domestic manufacture and assembly. It would also result in a net decrease of the foreign exchange burden. Some of this could be done within the context of the New Zealand–Australia Free Trade Area. Eventually, it may be feasible to reduce the number of models and makes assembled locally and to roll back domestic content to a level where the cost premium can be brought to below 60 percent.

# IX

## CHANGES IN THE STRUCTURE
## OF THE INDUSTRY

114.  Major adversities in the supply structure of automotive sectors in protected infant economies are high costs, a continuing foreign exchange burden, a growing technological gap, and other forces that undermine future growth. Measures to improve the economic efficiency of this industry must deal with these structural difficulties. The fundamental obstacle of economies of scale may be overcome in part by rationalizing production for internal markets. But major gains are also to be found by increasing economies of scale through specialized production for world markets. For this second alternative, participation in international industrial complexes manufacturing and marketing automotive products is an obvious course.

### DISADVANTAGES OF PROTECTION

115.  The development of automotive industries under systems of protection and progressive autarky has had, to varying degrees, at least four major adverse effects. To begin with, relative costs of production have been high by international standards. A rough estimate of the cost of the added resources employed in manufacturing automotive products in developing economies is somewhere in the neighborhood of $1.3 billion annually.[1] In effect, it costs developing countries about $2.1 billion in domestic resources to manufacture about

---

[1] Average international cost per vehicle is estimated at approximately $1,910 (12 million US-type vehicles at $2,000 per vehicle plus 11 million European-type vehicles at an estimated $1,800 per vehicle) plus $191 (10 percent *f.o.b.* price for freight and handling

$0.8 billion of internationally valued goods.[2] This is based upon an estimated average of 40 percent import content and an average 80 percent added manufacturing costs (Table 9). Overvaluation of the currency and the higher tax incidence would reduce somewhat this estimated cost premium to about $1.0 billion.[3]

TABLE 9:   Cost Premium for Manufacturing Automotive Products in Developing Economies, 1965

| Country | Production (units) | Import Content (percent)[a] | Cost Premium (f.o.b. world source = 1.0)[b] |
|---|---|---|---|
| Spain | 212,500 | 19 | 1.3* |
| Argentina | 196,800 | 31 | 2.6 |
| Brazil | 180,800 | 18 | 1.7 |
| Mexico | 126,700 | 49 | 1.6 |
| India | 69,500 | 41 | 2.0 |
| Venezuela | 53,500 | 92 | 1.6* |
| All other developing countries | 154,400 | 79 | 2.0* |
| Total | 994,200 | — | — |
| Weighted averages | | 40 | 1.8 |

[a] Percentages estimated from base figures for domestic content given in Annex Table 8 and adjusted upward an additional 15 percent for the import component of "domestic content."

[b] Ratios based upon conversions at official exchange rate. Figures marked with an asterisk (*) are estimates from pricing data.

*Source:* Tables 2 and 3, Annex Tables 1 and 8.

---

complete knocked-down units) equals an average $2,101 *c.i.f.* cost. (Average prices estimated from data in *Automotive News 1967 Almanac*.) Costs in developing countries average 80 percent above *f.o.b.* costs at an average 40 percent import content (Table 9), or an additional $1,528 per vehicle at a total cost of $3,438 per unit. This is an additional $1,337 per vehicle over *c.i.f.* cost ($2,101). For the one million vehicles manufactured and assembled in developing economies, this would mean $1.3 billion.

[2] From footnote 1, it cost on the average $3,438 to manufacture in a developing country a vehicle with a *c.i.f.* price of $2,101. Of this $3,438, import value is $1,260 (40 percent of $2,101, or $840, plus an estimated 50 percent duty on import content, or an additional $420). This leaves a residual of $2,178 cost of domestic value added. This means it cost $2,178 in domestic resources to manufacture $840 of internationally valued product, or about $2.60 for every $1.00 of internationally valued product, not taking into account differences in quality.

[3] If allowances were made for overvaluation of the currency (say 10 percent) and tax differentials per dollar of output at an estimated 14 percent (25.5 percent average taken for Brazil, Argentina, and Mexico less than the US average of 11.4 percent—see Table 3 footnotes) the resource cost difference of $1.3 billion would be reduced to about $1.0 billion (1.3 × .89 × .90).

67

116. Industrialization authorities often cite the social benefits of training an industrial labor force. But under a system of protection, in an industry producing at above international costs, the net gains from an upgrading of industrial skills may be more than offset by the net losses due to inefficient plant operations. Similarly, the backward linkage effects generated by assembly plants usually cited as beneficial, may actually give rise to a high-cost supply structure that is difficult to phase out at subsequent stages of industrialization. A second problem has been that, as production and consumption of automotive products have been allowed to expand, the foreign exchange burden has risen almost proportionally to the rate of sector expansion, even with the offsetting effect of progressive increases in domestic content. In Argentina, consumption of automotive products was allowed to expand under the illusion that import substitution would permit rapid growth at no extra cost in foreign exchange. In fact, foreign exchange costs rose from $42 million in 1959 to $126 million in 1965 (para. 81 and Table 7).

117. A third major problem of adjustment relates to the "technological gap." Because of the high cost of tooling up for low-volume production, developing countries usually end up with vehicle models and production techniques that lag behind latest developments. But since the costs of research and development are high, little or no effort is made to adapt product design and production techniques to low-volume production. Nor is enough effort made to develop indigenous research and development capabilities. This pattern has important implications for the future growth and development of the automotive industry; product proliferation associated with transplanted technology is not economic for domestic production, and obsolete products and techniques cannot compete in world markets.

118. A fourth major difficulty has been that once protection is built into a national economy, it is difficult to remove because of vested interests. The windfall profits possible under systems of protection and import substitution encourage the mushroom growth of small-scale, inefficient plants until markets become saturated. The higher the tariff wall, the more extensive the inefficient growth—as the case of Chile has demonstrated.[4] As domestic markets are saturated and competition intensifies, survival becomes progressively precarious.

---

[4] There were 7,800 vehicles manufactured in Chile in 1964 by 22 firms. High tariffs are indicated by relative prices—which range between 3.5 and 4.0 times the *c.i.f.* cost. Domestic content requirements (25 to 50 percent) are relatively high for this small number of vehicles. Installed capacity (29,600) was estimated at more than three times average annual output in 1964. See Leland L. Johnson, "Problems of Import Substitution: The Chilean Automobile Industry," *Economic Development and Cultural Change*, Vol. 15, No. 2 (January 1967), pp. 202–216.

Protection also dulls forces in the economy that could help develop more economic industries.[5] The high cost structures induced under protection have tended to price most industrial goods from developing countries out of world markets, thereby undermining any effort to solve the basic problem of scale through volume production for larger world markets. Protectionist interests also hinder the development of regional markets (see para. 125).

## POSSIBLE CHANGES IN MARKET STRUCTURE

119. The fundamental obstacle to production efficiency is the diseconomy of scale associated with production oriented to internal markets of limited size. Adjustment models must seek to overcome the scale disadvantage either through extending the size of the market or rationalizing production so as to achieve larger production runs. The former may be achieved through regionalism or specialized production for world markets. The latter may be realized by reducing the number of models and plants serving domestic markets.

120. A second major consideration in devising adjustment models is the foreign exchange burden. Models to improve sector efficiency should assure adequate growth at reasonable resource costs for foreign exchange savings. This may be achieved by reducing domestic content for the more expensive part of local procurement. In order to reduce domestic content to a level where the cost premium over US prices is within an acceptable range, it will be necessary to develop export capability to help pay for increased imported content. In the case of Brazil, average costs might be reduced 35 percentage points by replacing the more expensive engine and driveline parts (about 16 percent of vehicle value) with volume production for global markets.[6] This might be achieved through international manufacture and interchange systems outlined below.

121. Adjustment models should also include elements designed to narrow the technological gap, or at least assure that the gap is not widened.[7] Here again,

---

[5] Latin American scholars have indicated what might be termed an "alliance for stagnation" in countries that foster an uneconomic degree of domestic industries to advance technology and economic proficiency. See Claudio Veliz, editor, *Obstacles to Change in Latin America* (London: Oxford University Press, 1965).

[6] As indicated in Table 4, lines 5b and 7 under columns 6 and 7: 11 + 24 = 35 percentage points for 4 + 12 percent content.

[7] Discussions over the "technological gap" between the developing and developed countries have intensified in the past two years. In Latin America, a technological corollary to the Prebisch thesis has been emerging, arguing the need either to develop indigenous research and development capabilities or suffer the consequences of subservience to "technological imperialism" from industrialized areas. (See Victor L. Urquidi, "Latin American Development, Foreign Capital, and the Transmittal of Technology," *El Trimestre Económico* (January–March 1962). See also Celso Furtado, *Development and Underdevelopment* (University of California Press, 1964), pp. 60–62, 106–109.

corporations have an essential role in developing export capability in selected items. Even more important, international corporations can help build long-term industrial design and engineering capability into their overseas affiliates. Some share of the components and parts line manufactured by a developing country should adhere to international standards in design and specifications in order to develop the firm's earning capacity in the world economy. It may even prove expedient to develop dual product lines, one to fill domestic needs and the other to meet international standards. Export items also serve as a benchmark of quality and efficiency for industrial goods produced for the domestic market.

*Rationalization of Production for Domestic Markets*

122. National programs aimed at the standardization and interchangeability of components and parts can advance production efficiency through longer production runs. In some cases, more economic scales have been achieved through the use of consolidated assembly facilities for various models and makes or through the joint utilization of a parts manufacture plant to serve a broader range of equipment manufacturers. In Argentina, for example, automotive and aircraft equipment manufacturers (Kaiser and Lockheed) invested in joint ventures to manufacture axles and carburetors. Kaiser operated forging and casting facilities that also supply other equipment manufacturers. Some efforts have also been made to standardize major components (gearboxes, crankshafts, and transmissions) among Mexican equipment manufacturers (General Motors, Ford, and Chrysler), but with limited results. A rationalization program is much easier to build into an industrialization program from the outset than to implement after the industry is already established with its diversified product line.

123. Certain adjustments in vehicle designs would improve their functional utility under the different environmental conditions that prevail in developing countries.[8] The development by General Motors of the Holden for the Australian market is a case in point. There are, in fact, some revealing differ-

---

[8] Adjustments are needed to accommodate road conditions, climate, and the dearth of maintenance facilities. For example, among the features that would enhance utility in frontier areas are: higher ground clearance to avoid ruts in the road; added protection for the gas tank; a heavy-duty air cleaner for drier or dustier climates; a gasoline filter on intake spout; an oil pan shaped to maintain lubrication level at steeper incline (as on a farm tractor); a larger radiator with greater heat-dissipating capacity for hot climates; additional insulation for electrical systems against dampness and water; roll-down green wire mesh to keep out the insects at the window openings; and a lock on the hood and gas tank to prevent pilferage. (Data sheet provided by Richard Robinson of M.I.T.)

ences between American and European vehicle and engine design, which have obvious applications to the needs of consumers in developing economies.[9] American vehicle manufacturers are generally geared to diversity of, and rapid change in, product design (body sections redesigned annually with a complete change every three to five years and engine redesign every seven years). Model changes among European car-makers occur much less frequently. In the extreme, a firm like Citroën comes out with a revolutionary car every twenty-five years, with little or no change in between. Volkswagen also has remained competitive by standardizing and stabilizing design and tooling over an extended period. American consumers are more interested in power and ease of driving and maintenance than they are in initial costs and thermal efficiencies; European cars are less costly to purchase and operate, and may be designed to work for long periods of time (Volvo is a good example). Differences in income and fuel taxes account in part for these basic differences in consumer preferences. Smaller European engines require more frequent overhaul and replacement, particularly if overdriven, but service labor is cheaper in Europe.

124. A number of automotive manufacturers have designed truck bodies in order to decrease tooling costs for low-volume production. Substantial savings are possible through body designs that avoid contouring and require much less expensive equipment. Modular design principles based upon interchangeable body panels and the use of standardized mill forms for additional body and chassis elements also reduce production costs.[10] Berliet also simplified the front end of truck bodies manufactured in Algeria in order to reduce tooling costs. Tooling costs for small presses to bend sheet metal run about 5 to 10 percent of the heavy die presses needed to contour sheet metal. British Motor Corporation uses fiber glass bodies for manufacturing passenger cars in Chile.

*Regionalism and Barter Trade*

125. Much hope had been placed upon the development of regional markets as a means for improving production efficiency. The basic difficulty in implementing the Latin American Free Trade Area (LAFTA) agreement is that trading partners are anxious to sell but unwilling to buy. There are several other obstacles to implementing the LAFTA agreement. To begin with, national industries nurtured in a protectionist environment are opposed to

---

[9] See "Cars: The Continental Divide," *The Economist* (July 9, 1966).

[10] For example, Chrysler had designed the "LXV" for production in Turkey, Ford produces the "Bronco" in Argentina, and Kaiser the "KXM" in Argentina for this purpose. See Baranson, "Design for the Backwater," *Machine Design* (September 2, 1965), pp. 108–115. U.S. Steel has designed a series of vehicles based upon the use of standard steel mill forms, which reduces tooling and machining costs.

a lowering of internal tariffs. Furthermore, some countries are further along than others in national integration and the proliferation of supplier industries. Surface freight charges alone between countries like Argentina and Chile are a barrier. Differences in industrial development among member countries have been another major obstacle; for example, countries like Argentina and Chile are fearful of Brazilian competition based on its lower cost structure.

126.   Under the LAFTA Agreement, signed in 1961, internal tariffs and related restrictions were to be eliminated on "substantially" all products by 1973. Two mechanisms were created for the progressive liberalization of trade (known as "national list" and "general list" negotiations). One mechanism provides for the negotiation of bilateral concessions aimed at reducing average national tariffs 8 percent a year. These concessions are to be eventually extended to all LAFTA members. Under the second mechanism, every three years members agree to grant tariff concessions on a list of products representing one fourth of intra-LAFTA trade during the previous three-year period (to be applied cumulatively after 1973).

127.   The two developments that have occurred which affect the automotive field are complementarity agreements and the movement toward subregionalism. Under complementarity agreements, two countries agree to exchange certain components or specialize in given product categories. These plans are then formalized in intergovernmental agreements, permitting parts manufactured in one country to qualify as national content in another. A few such complementarity agreements have been negotiated since late 1965 between Argentina, Chile, and Mexico. These bilateral arrangements have been very limited in nature and, in fact, have increased production costs (see below), contrary to the basic intention of the LAFTA agreement. In its bilateral trading with Chile, Argentina has agreed to allow a limited interchange of components (up to 6 percent by Argentine vehicle value and not more than 30 percent of any one local item). The difficulty has been that whereas Argentina is able to export a few high-value items (such as engines, transmissions, and rear-axle assemblies), Chile is only able to export a large number of low-value items (such as air cleaners, wire harnesses, hub caps, and various forgings and castings). It has also been especially difficult to find items in Chile that come near Argentine quality and price.

128.   Automotive manufacturers have been frustrated time and again in their efforts to consolidate production facilities on a complementarity basis and trade in components and parts. There has been a permanent consultative group among Argentina, Brazil and Chile since 1963, but so far there have been

little or no results. For example Chile will not let Ford pick the most advantageous industry, but would rather have Ford develop a metal-working industry that Chile does not already have. Chile also objects to "resource-intensive" production in glass windows, rubber tires, or copper radiators. In 1966, Ford Argentina was sending engines to Chile and tried to find items such as copper radiators or certain castings that Chile can export advantageously in return. Certain foundry items cost as much as $5.50 in Chile, as compared to $1.60 in Argentina. With the high freight charges, a part supplied from Chile had to be priced substantially below Argentine costs to compete in the Argentine market. Argentina, on its side, does not want to allow Ford to phase out existing supply sources all at once, but rather 20 percent at a time. The result, if implemented, would be self-defeating, with two sources of supply and increased production costs in both Argentina and Chile.

129. Negotiations on lowering trade barriers between Argentina and Brazil began in November 1967, but Argentine manufacturers are fearful of the more efficient Brazilian parts manufacturers. Cost disparities are probably attributable to differences in the tariff and exchange structure, rather than to any significant differences in technical capabilities or market opportunities (para. 54). It is proposed to initiate interchange at the 15 percent level and move to 30 percent within five years (in place of the 6 percent limit imposed on Argentine trade with Chile). Large firms in competitive positions have strong incentives to liberalize trade between the two countries because of mounting investment costs.

130. In May 1967, a proposal was made to form a subregional Andean group consisting of Venezuela, Colombia, Chile, Peru, Ecuador, and Bolivia. Under the proposed arrangements, there would be a duty-free trade in the components program. Venezuela has held up signing the proposed agreement. But the fact is that the Andean market (about 100,000 vehicles) is half the size of Argentine demand. The subregional market is preferable to six more national industries, but integration into the larger LAFTA market would be even more advantageous in terms of overall economic efficiency.

131. The LAFTA vehicle market may be expected to double by 1975, providing a market for about 1,125,000 vehicles. At the well-known and widely accepted optimum of 240,000 units a year of a single basic vehicle type, this would mean no more than five major manufacturing complexes throughout the LAFTA region. But in fact average runs are somewhere around 10,000 and, as we have seen, costs are already well above import costs. The most that can be said at present is that the economic rationalization of automotive production will entail a reversal of the trend toward further atomization of

73

production facilities and proliferation of models, makes, and vehicle components.[11]

*International Specialization*

132. For newly industrializing economies, there are obvious advantages in certain lines of specialization. Relevant considerations include the level of technical sophistication demanded in manufacturing, the related manpower requirements, and whether significant diseconomies of scale can be avoided. Such specialization might include the production of trucks and buses, which are characteristically low-volume items, or specialized production of less-sophisticated parts that require disproportionate amounts of hand labor, such as bus assembly or the manufacture of low-volume sand castings. Economies of scale are more pronounced in metal stamping and the forging or machining of parts, where mechanized or automated equipment can be used, than in assembly or finishing operations requiring a minimum of machine tools or equipment. Diseconomies of small-scale production vary according to the industrial environment. Japan is a striking example of the ability to organize smaller-scale, labor-intensive activities at competitive costs.[12]

133. Precedents for reorganization along this line are to be found in Canada and Mexico. The US–Canadian Automotive Agreement provided for the expansion of Canadian car and component manufacture for the US market as a precondition for US firms continuing to sell assembled cars and trucks in Canada under a trade preference arrangement.[13] In Mexico an agreement was

---

[11] This theme of regionalism is expanded in Baranson, "Integrated Automobiles for Latin America," *Finance and Development* (IBRD, December 1968), pp. 25–29.

[12] See Baranson, *Manufacturing Problems in India*, pp. 66–69, and K. Kawamata, "The Automobile Industry and Current Problems," *Keidanren Review*, Vol. 2, No. 7 (1967), pp. 29–37.

[13] Under the US–Canadian Automotive Agreement, implemented in January 1965, the Canadian trade deficit in automotive trade with the USA has been reduced from US $578 million (1964) to $239 million (1967). Included here are passenger cars, trucks, buses, chassis, and automotive parts and accessories.

| | Imports to Canada | Exports from Canada (US $ million) | Canadian Trade Balance |
|---|---|---|---|
| 1964 | 654.1 | 75.9 | −578.2 |
| 1967 | 1,801.2 | 1,562.0 | −239.2 |

*Source:* US Bureau of Census, Foreign Trade Series. In 1968 Canadian automotive exports exceeded the $2 billion mark. The pro's and con's of the US–Canadian Agreement are summarized in Paul Wonnacott, "Canadian Automotive Protection: Content Provisions, the Bladen Plan, and Recent Tariff Changes," *Canadian Journal of Economics and Political Science*, Vol. XXXI, No. 1 (February 1965), pp. 98–115.

signed with Massey-Ferguson to manufacture tractors at 70 percent domestic content and cover the 30 percent import deficit with re-exports to the international firm's other overseas plants. Another program has been initiated by Chrysler to specialize by interchanging engines between its Mexican affiliate and North American plants.

134.  If developing countries are to move into more specialized production for world markets, industrialized countries will need to lower their trade barriers to permit two-way and multilateral trade. The US–Canadian agreement provides a model for such arrangements. Trade access to the EEC and EFTA areas would be especially appropriate for countries like Spain and Yugoslavia. Trade unions in industrialized countries are bound to raise objections to the location of production facilities abroad, unless such arrangements are viewed in the larger context of world growth and development. A narrower, short-term view would focus erroneously upon the loss of jobs to the industrialized countries. Reallocation of the international division of labor along the lines indicated in this study will benefit greatly the developing countries.[14]

135.  Technical and commercial requirements on export products are more stringent than those on production for domestic markets. The marketing of a Brazilian Volkswagen is no small task, and the international manufacturer has his trade name to protect. The systems of tariffs and subsidies upon which manufacturing costs and sales prices are founded in developing countries are precarious ground on which to base an international manufacturing operation. Most firms also have basic policies to keep products and components at international standards. In many cases, original equipment manufacturers have either had difficulties in getting their home country suppliers to locate abroad, or else their overseas supplier is unwilling to keep up with new component requirements for new vehicle models.

136.  There is also the matter of reliability of the supplier source under an international manufacturing and marketing system. A hostile bureaucracy can very easily shatter any chances for developing a manufacturing specialization for an international market. In 1959, Volkswagen tried to market 300 pas-

---

[14] For policy recommendations on accommodations to developing countries by industrialized nations, see Harry G. Johnson, *Economic Policies Toward Less Developed Countries* (Frederick A. Praeger, 1964). Professor Johnson outlines proposals for enlarging export opportunities within the GATT framework (pp. 129–135), details means to accord preferential entry of industrial products into the markets of industrialized countries (pp. 163–211), and recommends "maximum inducement to the less developed countries to modify their policies of currency overvaluation and import substitution to which they are addicted and to concentrate their efforts instead on economic development through trade with the rest of the world" (p. 245).

senger cars in the United States from its Brazilian subsidiary in order to overcome a temporary production bottleneck in Germany and to earn foreign exchange to pay for parts imports into Brazil. The shipment was stopped by the customs authorities, on the grounds that "Brazilian plants were not established for the convenience of American markets."[15] Similar incidents have been reported involving the levying of excise taxes and other procedural delays designed to thwart efforts to earn foreign exchange through the export of parts.

137. Economies operating under an import substitution regime have typically used a combination of tariff protection and exchange rate policies to subsidize domestic industry at the expense, eventually, of the export sector (except for those "non-traditional" exports which are also subsidized). The general pattern has been to lag the exchange rate behind domestic price increases and to apply the overvalued rate to inhibit "non-essential" imports. Favored industries are subsidized by export bonuses and special exemptions from tariffs on imported components and parts. Protection required to sustain domestic industries, coupled with overvaluation, inhibits the expansion of exports by increasing the internal cost structure and thus the price of exports on world markets. The industrial reorientation proposed in this study calls for development of export capability and replacement of high-cost manufacture in order to compete in world markets. Once the opportunities for import substitution have been exhausted and domestic markets saturated, a revised exchange policy may be needed before moving on to the next growth plateau based upon larger external markets. At this stage, devaluation accompanied by tariff reduction and the relaxation of restrictive controls will also help the badly needed price mechanisms restore efficient resource utilization.[16]

---

[15] See Claude McMillan and Richard F. Gonzalez, *International Enterprise in a Developing Economy* (Michigan State University, 1964), pp. 114–115. There was also considerable concern in Brazil about local reaction to the much lower than domestic price proposed for the export units.

[16] Devaluation is only effective to the degree that one or more of the following conditions prevail:

i) The rising internal price trend does not wipe out improvements in relative prices externally. Price rises may occur as a result of (a) the increased cost of imports, (b) the increased cost of domestic goods diverted to increased export demands (cost increases depending in part upon supply elasticities), and (c) increases in wage demands in response to the rise in domestic prices.

ii) Productivity gains during the adjustment period exceed price rises. These may occur as a result of a shift from less efficient protected industries serving domestic markets to more efficient export industries.

iii) Tariffs are adjusted downward in combination with devaluation in order to minimize increases in domestic prices induced by higher import costs and at the

# POTENTIAL LINES OF SPECIALIZATION

138. Specialization by developing countries in the manufacture of components or particular product lines for export to world markets merit consideration (a) where production runs are small by international standards (such as in heavy trucks or specialized vehicles); (b) where there is a low bulk-to-value ratio (as in axles and transmissions) so that transport charges may be absorbed in the relatively high value of the traded part;[17] (c) where there is a disproportionately high requirement for labor (as in sand castings, bus body-building, or in the manufacture of machine tools); (d) where a product or part is being phased out by the foreign partner and there is a need to maintain production of spare parts or a special type vehicle; or (e) where the international firm has a production expansion problem in the home country (labor or capital shortages) matched by a production expansion capability in the manufacturing affiliate country.

## *Export of Assembled Vehicles*

139. Several firms have used overseas plants for regional sales. Chrysler consolidated its manufacturing of right-wheel drives in Australia for sale to the Commonwealth market. Daimler-Benz exports buses from India to South Vietnam, Laos and Malaysia.[18] On a sales contract for 250 buses to Ceylon, the Indian affiliate of Daimler-Benz was able to make a bid only five percent above the German price (at the devalued rupee rate). This was the combined result of transport cost advantages and a devalued rupee.[19] (India

---

      same time to increase overall efficiency in the economy by weeding out marginal industries.

  iv) Fiscal and monetary management compensates for the inflationary and income distribution effects of devaluation and, along with measures to maintain or increase the new flow of external resources, manages to maintain a satisfactory level of foreign exchange reserves.

[17] Certain items may be more advantageous to make locally than others. For example, on automobile stampings, freight costs are quite high because it is not possible to "nest" most stamped body parts, so they have to be crated separately.

[18] These sales were conditioned by US AID procurement policies which require 90 percent American content. Special exemptions are granted to industrial goods manufactured in developing countries. Thus, Daimler-Benz can sell its Indian truck to Vietnam, but not the one manufactured in Germany.

[19] Prior to devaluation, the rupee was valued at Rs 4.75 to the dollar; after devaluation, Rs 7.50 to the dollar. Rupee prices have risen about 20 percent since devaluation. The net result is that a truck that sold for Rs 16,740 in the Indian market, or $3,600 at the old rate now sells for about Rs 20,040 or $2,730 at the new rate.

has long been competitive with the UK on bicycle tires sold to Burma or Japan.)

140. Several European truck manufacturers have considered transferring certain assembly and manufacturing lines to Latin America, to make room for newer models in home plants and at the same time provide an advantageous marketing wedge in Latin America. Bolinder Munktell of Sweden indicated a willingness to relocate certain agricultural equipment lines in developing countries for sale in world markets. In Algeria, for example, where quality and cost of metal work are favorable, bulky equipment requiring large amounts of hand-welding might be produced economically. Renault has designed a completely new car for manufacture in Brazil and export within and outside Latin America. It is adapted to the rougher roads and poorer servicing facilities that characterize hinterland areas. Cummins Engine (US) has concluded that a light-weight diesel engine with fuel economy features and low-initial cost designed for the small truck and bus market in Mexico might also find wider application in the stop-and-go delivery truck markets of North America and in a new line of passenger cars in the UK.

*Exports of Components and Parts*

141. Automotive firms have procured a limited number of parts in developing economies. In most cases, it has been a matter of providing a manufacturing affiliate with foreign exchange to help pay for needed imports. India furnishes fuel injector nozzles and pump elements to a German manufacturer. Housings for railroad car bearings are supplied by Egypt to the Fiat industrial complex in Italy on a barter basis; and injection pumps, spark plugs and insulators are procured in Brazil for assembly plants in India and Germany. Procurement of this kind has been prompted by supply shortages or production bottlenecks or by the advantage of phasing out the production of low-volume items in the home market. In many cases, the placement of foreign procurement orders in countries such as India and Brazil is a device for providing foreign exchange for required imports (or an indirect device for remitting profits through special pricing). For example, textiles and fibers have been purchased in India for the manufacture of European automotive parts. Up until now, such trading has been marginal. But the items cited indicate that some industrial goods can meet international standards.

142. There are other examples of foreign procurement which have been an outgrowth of barter arrangements to overcome foreign exchange difficulties. Volvo signed an agreement in 1959 with the Norwegian Government to buy

castings in Norway to pay for the import of 3,000 heavy trucks (about three million US dollars worth). A Portuguese concessionaire, on his own initiative, persuaded Volvo to procure certain castings, which were price competitive and of excellent quality. The concessionaire used exchange earnings from these exports to obtain additional import licenses for the purchase of Volvo cars and trucks. There is also now a two-way interchange of products and parts between Spain (Citroën) and Yugoslavia (TOMOS). Yugoslavia ships locks, cables and window rollers to Spain in return for Spanish-made Citroëns. The Perkins affiliate in India imports bearings and pistons from Yugoslavia to avoid hard currency expenditures in the UK. Scania Vabis has investigated the possibility of importing from Brazil wheel castings, instruments, and transmissions for assembly in Swedish trucks. They have also found that bus bodies are cheaper to manufacture in Brazil than in Sweden, because of lower labor costs on limited series. In Brazil, tooling dies for stamping truck body panels also cost one-fourth of the Swedish procurement price.

143.   There are several other examples of efforts to develop manufactured goods for export. The Indian affiliate of an American diesel manufacturer requested permission to expand production of crankshafts for export. The small scale of production necessary to meet local requirements (500 to 1,000) meant a prohibitively high unit cost; but with production at the 10,000 volume level, to help meet the global demand of the international manufacturer, costs would be competitive. The Indian plant is now producing at 70 percent domestic content, and the export of crankshafts would pay for a considerable portion of the remaining 30 percent import content. Volkswagen has explored the idea of reconditioning used engines, for which there is a substantial world market, either in Spain or Mexico.

## A NEW ROLE FOR INTERNATIONAL CORPORATIONS

144.   Competition in world markets requires a combination of resources and ability in manufacturing, marketing, research and engineering. Firms in newly industrializing economies generally lack the resources and skills to develop competitive products, efficient techniques, and the distribution and servicing systems necessary to market products abroad. Typically, developing countries encounter an overriding difficulty in gaining product acceptance in world markets, even after they have attained certain technical standards and a competitive price. This is in part a problem of psychological acceptance, and in part a question of the scale and resources necessary to invest in a worldwide distribution system.

79

145.    Partnership with international firms is one obvious answer.[20] There are several potential advantages. International firms are in a position to help developing countries redesign their components and vehicles for domestic and regional markets and expand their production capacities. Of even greater potential benefit, they possess the full range of resources and capacities to enable the developing country to enter world markets. Many international firms are willing to incur the additional difficulties and costs of using the manufacturer in a developing country as the supplier for the global market, provided they can thereby increase their world market share and net earnings. Most firms would prefer a program in this direction to more import substitution. Several firms have given serious consideration to the development of international manufacturing and interchange systems based upon national specialization in components or product lines. There are numerous possibilities: (a) the manufacture of specialized components and parts, (b) responsibility for a particular vehicle line, (c) specialization in low-volume replacement parts for obsolete models, or (d) the reconditioning of engines and parts.[21]

146.    The economic interests of the developing country can best be served by obtaining the long-term commitment of their industrial partners. International firms need to analyze product demands in developing countries and decide whether or not they want to stay in the market. If the decision is made to stay, most firms cannot afford to spread their capital and human resources too thinly in too many small and different marketing-manufacturing environments. It may be necessary to concentrate on the more promising markets and regions. It will be necessary to plan for the recruiting and training of personnel for the overseas staffing of the chosen manufacturing affiliates. Too often these operations are treated as stepchildren. Production engineering, procurement, and corporate financing are among the basic functions that need to be transplanted. Overseas operations require the development of new functions such as the handling of knocked-down units for overseas assembly plants (see para. 36). As the need to re-export from the overseas plant develops, the demands become even more exacting. Long-term arrangements with international firms should probably make provision for the establishment of a research and development capability.

---

[20] An expanded role for multi-national corporations is also stressed in Kleu, *South African Automotive Industry*, pp. 497–98.

[21] Replacement parts was a $9 billion business in the United States in 1964, with about 70 percent in the hands of independent manufacturers. 25 percent of this market was for "remanufactured" parts. See "Auto Parts Industry Gaining New Mileage," *New York Times*, November 29, 1964.

# SUGGESTIONS FOR FURTHER WORK

147.  The findings that emerge from this study apply largely to countries that have gone through substantial periods of industrialization under a system of protection and import substitution and are now seeking ways and means to phase out manufacturing activities that are uneconomic by competitive standards in world markets. Countries like New Zealand, Brazil and Argentina have pushed the limits of economic import substitution. The findings and recommendations may also be applied to countries that are now embarking upon industrialization programs and are interested in finding a more economic approach to import substitution. Small market economies should think twice before embarking upon even assembly operations, let alone more ambitious parts manufacture in depth. Countries such as Switzerland and Denmark have managed very well hitherto without extensive automotive manufacturing sectors.

148.  *Japan's role in automotive sector development.* Field work on Japan's potential role in assisting developing countries to enter world markets should prove advantageous. Japan now exports over 10 percent of its output and has at least 50 vehicle manufacturing and assembly affiliates in over 20 countries. The Japanese industry's success in adapting low-volume techniques among domestic suppliers in the home market and their reputation for designing low-cost functional vehicles should also have important application for developing countries. This might include a study of manpower needs for adapting and absorbing an industrial transplant, based upon the Japanese experience of technical assistance to supplier industries. Japan's decisions to emphasize truck production initially and hold back private consumption of passenger cars and public expenditures on roads, investing instead in rail transport for heavy passenger loads, are also instructive.

149.  A study might usefully be undertaken for a country like Brazil,[22] where the limits of import substitution have been reached in the automotive sector. The recommendations contained in this chapter might serve as a point of departure. A major purpose of such a study would be to work out concrete adjustment plans designed to: (a) reduce production costs without increasing the foreign exchange burden and (b) upgrade Brazil's indigenous design and

---

[22] The Brazilian Government was already considering proposals in 1967 to cut back domestic content requirements in order to reduce production costs. But, assuming unchanged consumption, this will mean increased foreign exchange costs (as much as US$50 million for a 10 percentage point decrease in domestic content on 200,000 vehicles) and the equivalent loss of national income and employment unless compensatory programs and market opportunities are worked out.

engineering abilities and thereby decrease Brazil's technological dependence upon foreign partners (see para. 121). Cost reduction and exchange targets should be worked out in conjunction with firms. The aim would be to develop a sector plan that would be both economically advantageous and commercially viable, and that at the same time would provide income and employment in the more efficient range of automotive production.

150. Further practical research might usefully be undertaken for countries either embarking upon programs to establish an automotive sector or considering a substantial expansion of present activities. This study provides an analytical framework for establishing cost parameters of domestic production and for devising programs to keep production within economic limits. Such studies would be appropriate in countries such as Colombia, Korea, or Turkey, where sector development or expansion programs are now being formulated. Recommendations might be in part a set of enjoinders on how *not* to proceed in developing the automotive industry. The approach to more efficient organization of the industry can serve as a model for other equipment sectors.

# ANNEX TABLES

ANNEX TABLE 1:   World Automotive Production by Country, 1965

| | Total | Cars | Trucks & Buses |
|---|---|---|---|
| *Developed Countries* | | | |
| United States | 11,112,000 | 9,335,000 | 1,777,000 |
| West Germany | 3,055,700 | 2,794,800 | 260,900 |
| United Kingdom | 2,134,900 | 1,691,100 | 443,800 |
| Japan | 1,870,500 | 696,800 | 1,173,700 |
| France | 1,581,600 | 1,364,000 | 217,600 |
| Italy | 1,158,200 | 1,090,600 | 67,600 |
| Canada | 849,000 | 708,000 | 141,000 |
| Belgium* | 443,600 | 418,400 | 25,200 |
| Australia | 352,900 | 304,800 | 48,100 |
| Sweden | 204,000 | 178,500 | 25,500 |
| South Africa* | 176,200 | 129,000 | 47,200 |
| Netherlands* | 75,100 | 62,200 | 12,900 |
| New Zealand* | 71,900 | 58,700 | 13,100 |
| Ireland* | 50,000 | 38,000 | 12,000 |
| Denmark* | 33,000 | 28,000 | 5,000 |
| Other countries[a] | 48,300 | 32,300 | 16,000 |
| Subtotal | 23,216,900 | 18,930,200 | 4,286,600 |
| | | | |
| *Developing Countries* | | | |
| Spain | 212,500 | 142,300 | 70,200 |
| Argentina | 196,800 | 131,800 | 65,000 |
| Brazil | 180,800 | 101,500 | 79,300 |
| Mexico | 126,700 | 88,700 | 38,000 |
| India | 69,500 | 23,100 | 46,400 |
| Venezuela* | 53,500 | 37,700 | 15,800 |
| Portugal | 37,000 | 30,000 | 7,000 |
| Malaysia | 25,000 | 25,000 | – |
| Iran | 8,900 | 6,300 | 2,600 |
| Other countries[b] | 84,500 | 38,400 | 46,100 |
| Subtotal | 995,200 | 624,800 | 370,400 |

|  | Total | Cars | Trucks & Buses |
|---|---|---|---|
| *Communist Countries* | | | |
| Soviet Union | 616,000 | 196,000 | 420,000 |
| East Germany | 110,000 | 95,000 | 15,000 |
| Czechoslovakia | 99,700 | 77,700 | 22,000 |
| Poland | 60,600 | 26,400 | 34,200 |
| Yugoslavia | 45,500 | 35,900 | 9,600 |
| Rumania | 22,800 | 7,000 | 15,800 |
| Hungary | 7,100 | – | 7,100 |
| Subtotal | 961,700 | 438,000 | 523,700 |
| Grand Total | 25,173,800[c] | 19,993,000 | 5,180,700 |

*Note:* There are several discrepancies among production figures because of differences in sources used. In some cases, figures represent projected estimates rather than actual production.

[a] Includes: Austria, Finland, Greece, Israel, Switzerland, and Rhodesia.

[b] Includes: Latin America—Peru, Colombia, Costa Rica.

      Asia—Thailand, Pakistan, Taiwan, Burma, South Korea.

      Middle East/Africa—United Arab Republic, Algeria, Morocco, Turkey,

              Nigeria, Ivory Coast, Malagasy.

[c] Totals include an undetermined number of unassembled vehicles exported and therefore double counted—say 20 percent of the export estimate of 3.9 million vehicles. The true grand total of world production is thus estimated at 24,329,000 for 1965.

\* Less than 50% domestic manufacture.

*Sources:* McGraw-Hill, *World Automotive Market Survey, 1966*, Automotive Manufacturers Association, Inc., World Motor Vehicle Data, 1965, Chambre Syndicale des Constructeurs d'Automobiles-*Repertoire Mondial des Usines d'Assemblage de Vehicules Automobiles*, Vols. I & II, July 1966.

ANNEX TABLE 2:  Motor Vehicle Registration,[a] 1950–67

('000)

| As of January 1 | Registered Vehicles[a] | | | | | |
|---|---|---|---|---|---|---|
| | 1950 | 1955 | 1960 | 1965 | 1966 | 1967 |
| Africa | 1,115 | 1,700 | 2,424 | 3,171 | 3,217 | 3,325 |
| Asia | 703 | 2,008 | 3,453 | 8,675 | 10,368 | 12,131 |
| Other America | 1,723 | 2,829 | 4,087 | 6,651 | 7,388 | 8,126 |
| Subtotal | 3,541 | 6,537 | 9,964 | 18,497 | 20,973 | 23,582 |
| USA | 43,774 | 58,050 | 71,502 | 86,309 | 90,361 | 94,177 |
| Canada | 2,195 | 3,565 | 4,941 | 6,225 | 6,511 | 6,762 |
| Western Europe | 8,500 | 14,447 | 25,257 | 45,522 | 50,709 | 55,302 |
| Oceania | 1,617 | 2,567 | 3,326 | 4,472 | 4,711 | 4,900 |
| Subtotal | 50,086 | 78,629 | 105,026 | 142,528 | 152,292 | 161,141 |
| Total[b] | 59,627 | 85,166 | 114,990 | 161,025 | 173,265 | 184,723 |

| | Average Annual Growth Rate, percent | | | | | |
|---|---|---|---|---|---|---|
| | 1950–55 | 1955–60 | 1960–65 | 1965–66 | 1966–67 | 1950–67 |
| Africa | 8.8 | 7.4 | 5.5 | 1.5 | 3.4 | 6.6 |
| Asia | 23.0 | 11.5 | 20.0 | 19.5 | 17.0 | 18.2 |
| Other America | 10.4 | 7.6 | 10.2 | 11.1 | 10.0 | 9.6 |
| Sub-group average | 13.0 | 8.8 | 13.2 | 13.4 | 12.4 | 11.8 |
| USA | 5.8 | 4.3 | 3.8 | 4.7 | 4.2 | 4.6 |
| Canada | 10.2 | 6.8 | 4.7 | 4.6 | 3.9 | 6.8 |
| Western Europe | 11.2 | 11.8 | 12.5 | 11.4 | 9.1 | 11.6 |
| Oceania | 9.7 | 5.3 | 6.1 | 5.3 | 4.0 | 6.7 |
| Sub-group average | 7.0 | 6.0 | 6.3 | 6.9 | 5.8 | 6.4 |
| Total[b] | 7.4 | 6.2 | 7.0 | 7.6 | 6.6 | 6.9 |

[a] Includes cars, trucks and buses.

[b] Does not include USSR, Yugoslavia, Czechoslovakia, East Germany, Poland, Hungary and Rumania with total registrations of 6,537,400 at January 1, 1967. (Automobile Manufacturers Association, Inc., *World Motor Vehicle Data 1966*.)

*Source:* Calculated from data in McGraw-Hill, *World Automotive Market Survey*, 1966 and 1967.

86

**ANNEX TABLE 3:** **Vehicle Density per Inhabitant, 1965**

| Country | Inhabitants per Vehicle |
|---|---|
| United States | 2.2 |
| Canada | 3.0 |
| Australia | 3.0 |
| New Zealand | 3.1 |
| Sweden | 4.0 |
| France | 4.6 |
| United Kingdom | 5.0 |
| West Germany | 5.5 |
| Belgium | 6.1 |
| Italy | 8.4 |
| Argentina | 14.5 |
| Japan | 15.5 |
| Venezuela | 17.5 |
| Spain | 26.5 |
| Portugal | 28.0 |
| Mexico | 37.8 |
| Brazil | 41.1 |
| Malaysia | 50.5 |
| Greece | 58.0 |
| Yugoslavia | 77.3 |
| India | 479.3 |

*Sources:* International Monetary Fund, *International Financial Statistics*, January 1967; Automobile Manufacturers Assoc., *World Motor Vehicle Data*, 1965; McGraw-Hill, *1966 World Automotive Market Survey.*

**ANNEX TABLE 4:  World Automotive Production by Company Size, 1965**

| Total Production Output (millions) | Number of Firms | Total Output (millions) | Percent of World Production | Average Volume per Firm (to nearest thousand) |
|---|---|---|---|---|
| 3.1–5.7 | 2 | 8.8 | 36.5 | 4,400,000 |
| 0.5–1.6 | 9 | 7.7 | 32.0 | 856,000 |
| 0.2–0.4 | 14 | 3.6 | 14.9 | 257,000 |
| Below 0.2 | 293 | 4.0 | 16.6 | 14,000 |
| Totals and averages | 318[a] | 24.1 | 100.0 | 76,000 |
| *Passenger Cars* | | | | |
| 2.6–4.9 | 2 | 7.6 | 39.0 | 3,800,000 |
| 0.5–1.5 | 7 | 6.1 | 31.3 | 871,000 |
| 0.1–0.4 | 16 | 3.5 | 17.9 | 219,000 |
| Below 0.1 | 176[b] | 2.3 | 11.8 | 13,000 |
| Subtotals and averages | 201 | 19.5 | 100.0 | 97,000 |
| *Trucks and Buses* | | | | |
| 0.5–0.8 | 2 | 1.3 | 27.7 | 650,000 |
| 0.1–0.2 | 10 | 1.5 | 31.9 | 150,000 |
| 0.013–0.1 | 32 | 1.2 | 25.5 | 38,000 |
| Below 13,000 | 206[b] | 0.7 | 14.9 | 3,000 |
| Subtotals and averages | 250 | 4.7 | 100.0 | 19,000 |

*Note:* Excluding USSR and Eastern Europe.
[a] Subtotals add to more than total because some firms produce both cars and trucks.
[b] Estimated from source material available.
*Source:* Calculated from data in McGraw-Hill, *1966 World Automotive Market Survey.*

## ANNEX TABLE 5: World Automotive Production by Country and Leading Firms, 1965

### All Type Vehicles

| USA | Japan | UK | Germany | France |
|---|---|---|---|---|
| (1) General Motors 5,706,000 | (10) Toyota 477,700 | (6) BMC 854,300 | (4) Volkswagen 1,510,000 | (9) Renault 542,000 |
| (2) Ford Motors 3,113,000 | (14) Nissan 345,900 | (8) Ford 589,800 | (7) Opel 631,100 | (11) Citroën 465,000 |
| (3) Chrysler Corp. 1,611,000 | (18) Toyo Koggo 273,500 | (16) Vauxhall 333,200 | (15) Ford 334,500 | (17) Peugeot 293,000 |
| (13) American Motors 346,000 | | (21) Rootes 212,600 | (19) Daimler-Benz 236,900 | (20) Simca 230,000 |

| Canada | Italy | Australia | Belgium |
|---|---|---|---|
| (12) General Motors 419,000 | (5) Fiat 988,000 | (23) General Motors 165,200 | (24) Ford 161,730 |
| (22) Ford 211,000 | | | |
| (25) Chrysler 153,000 | | | |

### Cars

| USA | Japan | UK | Germany | France | Italy |
|---|---|---|---|---|---|
| (1) General Motors 4,949,000 | (15) Toyota 236,900 | (6) BMC 671,400 | (4) Volkswagen 1,415,300 | (9) Renault 470,000 | (5) Fiat 947,000 |
| (2) Ford Motors 2,566,000 | (20) Nissan 170,200 | (8) Ford 504,500 | (7) Opel 615,600 | (10) Citroën 380,000 | |
| (3) Chrysler Corp. 1,468,000 | | (17) Vauxhall 220,800 | (13) Ford 307,700 | (14) Peugeot 270,000 | |
| (12) American Motors 346,000 | | (18) Rootes 174,400 | (19) Daimler-Benz 174,000 | (16) Simca 230,000 | |
| | | (25) Standard-Triumph 120,000 | | | |

| Canada | Australia | Sweden |
|---|---|---|
| (11) General Motors 351,000 | (22) General Motors 142,600 | (24) Volvo 130,000 |
| (21) Ford 168,000 | | |
| (23) Chrysler 136,000 | | |

### Trucks

| USA | Japan | UK | Germany | Brazil |
|---|---|---|---|---|
| (1) General Motors 757,000 | (3) Toyota 240,900 | (5) BMC 183,200 | (13) Volkswagen 94,700 | (32) Willys 23,000 |
| (2) Ford Motors 547,000 | (4) Toyo Koggo 192,200 | (10) Bedford (Vauxhall) 112,400 | (19) Daimler-Benz 62,900 | |
| (7) International 171,000 | (6) Nissan 175,700 | (14) Ford 85,300 | (28) Ford 26,800 | **Spain** |
| (8) Chrysler Corp. 143,000 | (9) Diahatsu 137,500 | (26) Rootes 38,200 | (40) Opel 15,500 | (35) Citroën 20,500 |
| (12) Kaiser 106,000 | (11) Mitsubishi 110,500 | (29) Leyland 25,000 | (42) Rheinstahl-Hanomag 15,000 | |
| (31) White 25,000 | (18) Isuzu 57,700 | | (44) Magirus 13,000 | **Argentina** |
| (36) Mack 20,000 | (20) Fugi 54,600 | | | (37) IKA 18,600 |
| | (21) Honda 46,700 | **France** | **Canada** | |
| **Italy** | (22) Prince 44,600 | (15) Citroën 85,000 | (17) General Motors 68,000 | **India** |
| (24) Fiat 41,000 | (25) Suzuki 40,000 | (16) Renault 72,000 | (23) Ford 43,000 | (39) Tata Mercedes 17,000 |
| | (27) Aichi 33,400 | (33) Peugeot 23,000 | (38) Chrysler 17,000 | |
| | (31) Hino 24,800 | (41) Berliet 15,500 | | |
| **Australia** | | | | |
| (34) General Motors 22,600 | | | | |
| **Sweden** | | | | |
| (43) Volvo 15,000 | | | | |

*Note:* World ranking in group in parentheses.
*Source:* Compiled from data in McGraw-Hill, *1966 World Automotive Market Survey.*

**ANNEX TABLE 6: Automotive Assembly Lines in Operation throughout the World, July 1966**

| Country | Number of Assembly Lines in Operation | Number of Countries in which Assembly Lines Are Established |
|---|---|---|
| United States[a] | 122 | 26 |
| Great Britain | 64 | 27 |
| France | 62 | 26 |
| West Germany | 55 | 22 |
| Japan | 49 | 22 |
| Italy | 25 | 22 |
| Sweden | 10 | 8 |
| Total | 387 | 55 |

[a] Includes British, German and Australian affiliates.

*Source:* Chambre Syndicale des Constructeurs d'Automobiles, *Repertoire Mondial des Usines d'Assemblage de Vehicules Automobiles*, Vols. 1 & 11, July 1966.

## ANNEX TABLE 7: Growth in Automotive Production by Major Producing Countries, 1955–65

| | Production | | Annual Average Rate of Growth (*percent*) |
|---|---|---|---|
| | 1955 | 1965[a] | |
| *Developed Countries (except USSR and Eastern Europe)* | | | |
| Japan | 68,932 | 1,875,614 | 39.0 |
| Italy | 268,766 | 1,175,548 | 16.0 |
| Sweden | 50,299 | 205,717 | 15.2 |
| Netherlands | 19,339 | 36,061 | 13.7 |
| New Zealand[b] | 43,674 | 71,812 | 13.2 |
| West Germany | 908,702 | 3,055,700 | 12.9 |
| France | 725,083 | 1,616,153 | 8.3 |
| Canada | 452,114 | 855,476 | 6.7 |
| Australia | 218,004 | 407,596 | 6.7 |
| United Kingdom | 1,237,068 | 2,177,261 | 6.1 |
| USA | 9,204,049 | 11,137,830 | 1.9 |
| *USSR and Eastern Europe* | | | |
| Yugoslavia | 15,921[c] | 45,452 | 19.5 |
| Czechoslovakia | 24,183 | 90,713 | 14.3 |
| Poland | 17,000 | 60,550 | 13.7 |
| East Germany | 36,438 | 110,000 | 11.9 |
| USSR | 445,268 | 616,000 | 3.5[d] |
| *Developing Countries* | | | |
| Argentina | 32,830[e] | 194,536 | 35.0 |
| Spain | 30,436[e] | 228,935 | 29.0 |
| Brazil | 30,700[e] | 185,645 | 25.0 |
| Mexico | 32,275 | 96,654 | 11.7 |
| India | 30,854 | 69,500 | 8.7 |

[a] 1965 production figures differ slightly from those quoted in Table 1 from the McGraw-Hill source; the 1965 production figures here are taken from the AMA source in order to maintain the integrity of the comparisons in this table.

[b] For period 1960/61 to 1965/66.

[c] 1957.

[d] During an earlier period (1946–55), the rate of growth was 17.9%.

[e] 1959.

*Source:* Compiled and calculated from data in Automobile Manufacture Association, *World Motor Vehicle Data, 1965.*

**ANNEX TABLE 8:** Manufacturing and Assembly in Developing Countries, by Number of Firms and Domestic Content, 1965

| | Number of Firms | Domestic Content | Total[b] | Cars | Trucks and Buses |
|---|---|---|---|---|---|
| *Latin America* | | | | | |
| Argentina | 12 | 72–90 | 196,800 | 131,800 | 65,000 |
| Brazil | 11 | 95–100 | 180,800 | 101,500 | 79,300 |
| Mexico | 12 | 60 | 126,700 | 88,700 | 38,000 |
| Venezuela | 16 | 5–14 | 53,500 | 37,700 | 15,800 |
| Peru | 7 | 30 | 3,000 | 1,700 | 1,300 |
| Colombia | 5 | 25–40 | 2,800 | 300 | 2,500 |
| Costa Rica | 11 | a | 1,300 | 900 | 400 |
| Uruguay | 16 | 0–10 | n.a. | n.a. | n.a. |
| Subtotal | 90 | – | 564,900 | 362,600 | 202,300 |
| *Asia* | | | | | |
| India | 8 | 61–80 | 69,500 | 23,100 | 46,400 |
| Malaysia | 2 | 8–17 | 25,000 | 25,000 | – |
| Thailand | 7 | a | 15,900 | 6,900 | 9,000 |
| Pakistan | 4 | a | 9,800 | 1,800 | 8,000 |
| Taiwan | 3 | a | 3,900 | 2,400 | 1,500 |
| Burma | 2 | a | 1,800 | 1,200 | 600 |
| South Korea[c] | 1 | a | 1,500 | – | 1,500 |
| Indonesia | 4 | n.a. | n.a. | n.a. | n.a. |
| Subtotal | 31 | – | 127,400 | 60,400 | 67,000 |
| *Europe* | | | | | |
| Spain | 21 | 90–100 | 212,500 | 142,300 | 70,200 |
| Portugal | 23 | 25 | 37,000 | 30,000 | 7,000 |
| Subtotal | 44 | – | 249,500 | 172,300 | 77,200 |

*Annex Table 8, cont.*

| | Number of Firms | Domestic Content | Total[b] | Cars | Trucks and Buses |
|---|---|---|---|---|---|
| *Middle East/Africa* | | | | | |
| United Arab Republic | 2 | 30–45 | 12,200 | 8,500 | 3,700 |
| Algeria | 2 | 25 | 9,600 | 6,200 | 3,400 |
| Iran | 6 | 65 | 8,900 | 6,300 | 2,600 |
| Morocco | 5 | 30–50 | 7,500 | 6,200 | 1,300 |
| Turkey | 8 | a | 5,300 | – | 5,300 |
| Nigeria | 10 | n.a. | 5,000 | – | 5,000 |
| Ivory Coast | 1 | a | 2,200 | 1,100 | 1,100 |
| Malagasy | 2 | a | 1,700 | 1,200 | 500 |
| Subtotal | 36 | – | 52,400 | 29,500 | 22,900 |
| Grand Total | 201 | | 994,200 | 624,800 | 369,400 |

a Assembly only.

b Some of the "production" figures for the smaller countries including Malaysia actually represent planned capacity and should not be taken literally.

c Military vehicles only.

*Sources:* Chambre Syndicale des Constructeurs d'Automobiles, *Repertoire Mondial des Usines d'Assemblage de Vehicules Automobiles*, Vols. I & II, July 1966; McGraw-Hill, *1966 World Automotive Market Survey;* Automobile Manufacturers Association, *World Motor Vehicle Data, 1965.*

ANNEX TABLE 9: Estimated Production Cost by Domestic Content and Production Volume, Passenger Car, India, 1966

| Volume of Production per annum | Percentage Domestic Content | Cost per Unit (*rupees*) | Index of Cost (*car f.o.b. Europe = 100*)[a] |
|---|---|---|---|
| 3,000 | 28 | 7,778 | 152 |
| | 47 | 9,061 | 177 |
| | 60 | 10,444 | 204 |
| | 97 | 15,367 | 300 |
| 5,000 | 28 | 7,524 | 147 |
| | 47 | 8,477 | 166 |
| | 60 | 9,403 | 184 |
| | 97 | 12,750 | 249 |
| 5,700[b] | 85 | 11,320 | 220 |
| 8,000 | 28 | 7,381 | 144 |
| | 47 | 8,149 | 159 |
| | 60 | 8,817 | 172 |
| | 97 | 11,278 | 220 |
| 10,000 | 28 | 7,333 | 143 |
| | 47 | 8,039 | 157 |
| | 60 | 8,622 | 168 |
| | 97 | 10,788 | 211 |
| 12,000 | 28 | 7,301 | 143 |
| | 47 | 7,966 | 156 |
| | 60 | 8,492 | 166 |
| | 97 | 10,460 | 204 |

[a] The European ex-factory cost, pre-devaluation, 1966 was Rs. 5,118.
[b] Actual production April, 1966.
*Source:* Computed from data furnished by Indian manufacturer.

ANNEX TABLE 10:  Home Market versus Overseas Pricing, 1966[a]

| Home Country | UK | USA | France | Germany | Italy | Japan | Switzerland | Sweden | Netherlands | USSR |
|---|---|---|---|---|---|---|---|---|---|---|
| | | | | | Overseas Markets | | | | | |
| *United Kingdom* | | | | | | | | | | |
| BMC (MGB) | $ 2,436 | 106% | 134% | 127% | 127% | 188% | 115% | – | – | – |
| BMC (Mini) | 1,442 | 102 | 124 | 95 | 95 | 172 | 93 | – | – | – |
| Ford Anglia | 1,557 | 86 | 96 | – | 100 | – | 96 | – | – | – |
| Ford Cortina | 1,814 | 81 | 97 | 86 | 126 | 172 | 99 | – | – | – |
| Vauxhall Viva | 1,621 | – | 99 | 103 | 106 | 224 | 98 | – | – | – |
| Vauxhall Cresta | 2,965 | – | 129 | – | 126 | 178 | 104 | – | – | – |
| Rootes Hillman (Imp) | 1,509 | 99 | 108 | 94 | 110 | 228 | 97 | – | – | – |
| Jaguar E-type Roadster | 5,412 | 80 | 142 | 127 | 142 | 212 | 114 | – | – | – |
| Aston Martin DB6 Manual | 13,994 | 112 | – | 121 | 130 | – | – | – | – | – |
| *United States* | | | | | | | | | | |
| Ford Mustang | 222% | $2,876 | 215% | – | 198% | 319% | 172% | – | – | – |
| *France* | | | | | | | | | | |
| Citroën DS21 | 153% | 107% | $3,480 | 95% | 120% | 223% | 117% | – | – | – |
| Renault 10 | 122% | – | 1,599 | 94% | 100% | 199% | 108% | – | – | – |
| *Germany* | | | | | | | | | | |
| VW 1300 | 141% | 123% | 110% | $ 1,288 | 116% | 210% | 122% | – | – | – |
| Mercedes 200D | 203% | 144% | 134% | 2,878 | 144% | 250% | 135% | – | – | – |
| Mercedes 600 | 177% | 156% | 141% | 14,137 | 135% | 235% | 122% | – | – | – |
| Opel Kadett 2-D | – | 124% | 118% | 1,338 | 117% | – | 122% | – | – | – |
| Taunus 12M (Ford) | 162% | – | 117% | 1,422 | 112% | – | 125% | – | – | – |
| *Italy* | | | | | | | | | | |
| Fiat 500 | 138% | – | 126% | 101% | $ 829 | 241% | 109% | – | – | – |
| Fiat 1500 | 118% | – | 99% | 82% | 2,134 | 184% | 102% | – | – | – |
| Alfa Romeo (GSGT) | 145% | 115% | 128% | 109% | 3,668 | 174% | 107% | – | – | – |
| *Sweden* | | | | | | | | | | |
| Volvo 122S | 91% | 76% | 98% | 77% | 82% | 119% | 81% | $3,506 | – | – |
| Saab Sedan | 83% | 82% | 91% | 69% | 85% | 130% | 81% | 2,453 | – | – |
| *Netherlands* | | | | | | | | | | |
| Daf | 112% | – | 94% | 78% | 93% | – | 93% | – | $1,495 | – |
| *Japan* | | | | | | | | | | |
| Toyota Corona | 140% | 120% | – | – | – | $1,552 | – | – | – | – |
| *Soviet Union* | | | | | | | | | | |
| Moskvitch (408 Saloon) | 37% | – | 33% | – | – | 47% | 36% | – | – | $4,991 |

[a] Home markets retail price (including duties and taxes) in US dollars; all others as a percent of home market price.

Note: Dash (–) indicates model not sold or price data not available.
Source: The Economist, July 9, 1966, p. xxx.

95

Comparative Production Costs, US/India, Manufacture of a Diesel Engine, 1964

|                       | United States | United Kingdom | India   |
|-----------------------|:-------------:|:--------------:|:-------:|
| Engines per year[a]   | 14,000        | 3,000          | 1,200   |
|                       | *Dollar Costs*[c] |            |         |
| Labor                 | 212           | 206            | 120     |
| Materials             | 1,359         | 2,048          | 4,533   |
| Overhead[b]           | 529           | 732            | 1,379   |
| Total costs           | $2,100        | $2,986         | $6,032  |
| Capital/output ratio  | 0.61          | 0.79           | 3.02    |
| Overhead/labor ratio  | 2.47          | 3.55           | 11.25   |
|                       | *Percentages* |                |         |
| Labor                 | 10.1          | 6.9            | 2.0     |
| Materials             | 64.7          | 68.6           | 75.1    |
| Overhead              | 25.2          | 24.5           | 22.9    |
| Total costs           | 100.0         | 100.0          | 100.0   |

[a] This is for this engine series only—actually the scale difference factor based on value added was about 3.7 percent (see p. 95 in source cited below).

[b] Includes all other variable manufacturing costs and capital charges.

[c] Converted at Rs. 4.75 = $1.00.

*Source:* Jack Baranson, *Manufacturing Problems in India* (Syracuse University Press, 1967), p. 88.

**ANNEX TABLE 12: Argentina, Vehicle Production and Authorizations by Firms, 1965**

| Firm | Number of Models | Authorized Production | Actual Production | Percent Distribution | Production/ Authorization |
|---|---|---|---|---|---|
| Industrias Kaiser | 17 | 67,179 | 56,625 | 29.1 | 84.3 |
| Ford Motor | 6 | 31,475 | 30,424 | 15.6 | 96.7 |
| Fiat Concord | 5 | 28,985 | 28,868 | 14.8 | 99.6 |
| General Motors | 5 | 27,740 | 25,212 | 13.0 | 90.9 |
| Chrysler | 10 | 18,270 | 16,163 | 8.3 | 88.5 |
| Siam Di Tella[b] | 4 | 13,744 | 13,120 | 6.7 | 95.5 |
| S.A.F.R.A.R. | 2 | 8,490 | 6,647 | 3.4 | 78.3 |
| Industria Automotriz Santa Fe | 4 | 6,273 | 5,494 | 2.8 | 87.6 |
| Citroën | 3 | 8,279 | 4,687 | 2.4 | 56.6 |
| D.I.N.F.I.A. | 2 | 3,465 | 3,136 | 1.6 | 90.5 |
| Mercedes-Benz | 10 | 4,800 | 3,075 | 1.6 | 64.1 |
| Insard | – | 4,167 | 536 | 0.3 | 12.9 |
| Metalmecánica | – | 3,500[a] | 478 | 0.2 | 13.7 |
| Total | 68 | 226,367 | 194,465 | 100.0 | 85.9 |

[a] Includes 1,000 units of Simca Ariane.
[b] Merged with Industrias Kaiser Argentina in late 1965.
*Source:* Asociación de Fabricantes Argentinas (ADEFA), *Production.*

**ANNEX TABLE 13: Argentina, Plant Capacity and Utilization, Five Leading Firms, 1965**

| Firm | Annual Output (Cars & Trucks) | Capacity | Percent Utilization |
|---|---|---|---|
| Kaiser | 56,600 | one shift —27,600 | – |
| | | two shifts —55,200[b] | – |
| | | three shifts—92,800 | 61.0 |
| Ford | 30,400 | one shift —40,300 | 75.4 |
| Mercedes | 3,100 | one shift — 4,800 | 64.6 |
| | | two shifts — 7,200 | 43.1 |
| Fiat[a] | 28,900 | one shift —19,200 | – |
| | | two shifts —38,400 | 75.3 |
| | | three shifts—57,600 | 50.2 |
| Chrysler | 16,200 | one shift —19,000 | 85.3 |
| Averages | 27,040 | one shift (5 firms)—22,180 | 121.9 |
| | 29,500 | two shifts (3 firms)—33,600 | 87.9 |

[a] Some interchangeability among plant facilities for manufacturing vehicles, tractors and diesel motors.
[b] Author's estimate.
*Source:* Company reports.

# ANNEX TABLE 14: Argentina, Value Added, Fixed Assets, and Employment, 1963–64

| Category Measured | Ford | | Kaiser | | Mercedes-Benz | | Chrysler | | Fiat Concord | |
|---|---|---|---|---|---|---|---|---|---|---|
| | 1963 | 1964 | 1963 | 1964 | 1963 | 1964 | 1963 | 1964 | 1963 | 1964 |
| Vehicle output (units) | 9,333 | 25,264 | 20,274 | 50,042 | 1,648 | 2,222 | 8,291 | 12,776 | 18,229 | 24,093 |
| Fixed assets after depreciation (million pesos) | 6,181 | 5,795 | 3,351 | 3,718 | 1,823 | 2,052 | 2,595 | 2,890 | 2,814[a] | 3,993 |
| Value added (million pesos constant prices) | 877 | 2,296 | 4,580 | 6,409 | 543 | 753 | 1,588 | 1,577 | 3,101 | 3,045 |
| Employment (number employed) | 3,018 | 3,371 | 7,541 | 9,526 | 732 | 993 | 2,009 | 2,298 | 1,271 | 1,471 |
| Employees per million pesos value added (line 4 ÷ line 3) | 3.411 | 1.468 | 1.647 | 1.482 | 1.347 | 1.319 | 1.264 | 1.457 | 0.410 | 0.483 |
| Employees per unit output (line 4 ÷ line 1) | 0.323 | 0.133 | 0.372 | 0.190 | 0.444 | 0.447 | 0.242 | 0.180 | 0.070 | 0.061 |
| Value added in million pesos per unit output (line 3 ÷ line 1) | 0.094 | 0.091 | 0.226 | 0.128 | 0.300 | 0.339 | 0.192 | 0.123 | 0.170 | 0.126 |
| Fixed assets per value added (line 2 ÷ line 3) | 5.434 | 2.762 | 0.732 | 0.580 | 3.357 | 2.725 | 1.633 | 1.833 | 0.907 | 1.311 |
| Fixed assets in million pesos per unit output (line 2 ÷ line 1) | 0.511 | 0.251 | 0.165 | 0.074 | 1.106 | 0.923 | 0.313 | 0.226 | 0.154 | 0.166 |

[a] Estimate by author.

Sources: Special reports furnished to World Bank mission, December 1965; Annual Company Reports.

## ANNEX TABLE 15: Argentina, Price Comparisons, Automotive Parts, September 1965

| Part | USA | | | Argentina | | |
|------|-----|-----|-----|-----------|-----|-----|
| | Purchase Price (US$) | Freight, etc. USA to Buenos Aires (US$) | Price c.i.f. Argentina (US$) | Procurement Cost (M$N) | Procurement Cost (US$) | Argentine/ USA Price Comparison (US=100.0) |
| Engine assembly 6 cyl. | 330.20 | 86.63 | 419.83 | 143,222 | 588.65 | 167.6 |
| Transmission assembly | 57.35 | 30.40 | 87.75 | 17,823 | 99.57 | 173.6 |
| Rear axle | 57.08 | 30.25 | 87.33 | 27,050 | 151.11 | 264.7 |
| Starter assembly | 13.79 | 3.59 | 17.38 | 6,684 | 37.34 | 270.8 |
| Generator (12 volt) | 14.12 | 3.67 | 17.79 | 5,641 | 31.51 | 223.2 |
| Tire (15") | 9.86 | 5.23 | 15.09 | 4,369 | 24.41 | 247.6 |
| Wheel (15") | 2.40 | 1.27 | 3.67 | 1,050 | 5.87 | 244.6 |
| Piston | 1.43 | .37 | 1.80 | 714 | 3.99 | 279.0 |
| Radiator | 11.43 | 6.06 | 17.49 | 6,850 | 38.27 | 334.8 |
| Cylinder block | 38.05 | 9.89 | 47.94 | 17,317 | 96.74 | 254.2 |
| Crankshaft | 12.07 | 3.14 | 15.21 | 9,582 | 53.53 | 443.5 |
| Camshaft | 3.52 | .92 | 4.44 | 1,545 | 8.63 | 245.2 |
| Steering wheel | 2.52 | 1.34 | 3.86 | 1,420 | 7.93 | 314.7 |
| Distributor | 7.61 | 1.98 | 9.59 | 2,400 | 13.41 | 176.2 |
| Battery | 7.75 | 4.11 | 11.86 | 4,215 | 23.55 | 303.9 |
| Clutch | 9.01 | 4.78 | 13.79 | 4,057 | 22.66 | 251.5 |
| Fuel pump | 4.08 | 2.16 | 6.24 | 937 | 5.23 | 128.2 |
| Total | $585.27 | | | | $1,182.40 | 202.2 |

*Note:* For Rambler Custom 660.
*Source:* Special report furnished to World Bank mission, December, 1965.

## ANNEX TABLE 16: US/Argentina Vehicle Production Volume and Average Unit Costs, 1965

| | Output (units) | Unit Price (US$) | Total Cost to Economy (US$ millions) |
|---|---|---|---|
| *Argentina*[a] | | | |
| Total | 195,000 | 4,773[b] | 930.8 |
| Passenger cars | 135,000 | 4,642 | 626.7 |
| Trucks and buses | 60,000 | 5,068 | 304.1 |
| *United States* | | | |
| Total | 11,114,000 | 1,934 | 21,500 |
| Passenger cars | 9,329,000 | 1,919 | 17,900 |
| Trucks and buses | 1,785,000 | 2,017 | 3,600 |
| *Argentina/United States Ratios (US = 1.0)* | | | |
| Total | .018 | 2.5 | .043 |
| Passenger cars | .014 | 2.4 | .035 |
| Trucks and buses | .034 | 2.5 | .084 |

[a] US dollar figures are based upon the 1965 pesos value deflated to 1960 pesos and converted at the 1960 official exchange rate of 82.7 pesos to the dollar.

[b] Converting 1965 pesos at the 1965 rate, the average price per vehicle is $4,080.

*Source:* Automobile Manufacturers Association (USA), *Automobile Facts and Figures, 1965;* ADEFA; CONADE.

## ANNEX TABLE 17: Price Comparisons, USA/Argentina, 1965

*(US dollars)*

| | USA Domestic Price $ | Argentine Domestic Price[a] $ | Ratio Argentina/US (US=100) | Argentine Export Price[a] $ | Ratio Argentina/US (US=100) |
|---|---|---|---|---|---|
| *Kaiser Jeep (JA-2PB)* | | | | | |
| Advertised delivery price | 1,728 | 3,188 | 184 | 3,188 | 184 |
| Tax deletion | (119) | (656) | – | (1,042) | – |
| Tax-free price | 1,609 | 2,532 | 157 | 2,146 | 133 |
| Freight etc. USA-Argentina | 450 | – | – | – | – |
| Total | 2,059 | 2,532 | 123 | 2,146 | 104 |
| *Kaiser Rambler Classic (Custom 660)* | | | | | |
| Advertised delivery price | 2,256 | 6,423 | 285 | 6,423 | 285 |
| Tax deletion | (174) | (1,599) | – | (2,334) | – |
| Tax-free price | 2,082 | 4,825 | 232 | 4,089 | 196 |
| Freight etc. USA-Argentina | 550 | – | – | – | – |
| Total | 2,632 | 4,825 | 183 | 4,089 | 155 |

[a] Conversion rate 179 pesos = US$1.00.
*Source:* Company reports.


## ANNEX TABLE 18: Argentina, Corporate Earnings of Four Vehicle Manufacturers, 1964

| Firm | Net Profits (Losses)[a] | Sales | Shareholders' Equity[c] | Net Profit as Percent of Sales | Net Profit as Percent of Shareholders' Equity |
|---|---|---|---|---|---|
| | *(million pesos)* | | | | |
| Kaiser[b] | 1,203 | 26,766 | 5,427 | 4.5 | 22.1 |
| Ford | 1,031 | 16,779 | 3,756 | 6.1 | 27.4 |
| Mercedes-Benz | (95) | 3,766 | n.a. | −2.5 | n.a. |
| Fiat Concord | 1,010 | 7,355 | 5,501 | 13.7 | 18.4 |

n.a. = not available.
[a] After all taxes and interest charges.
[b] Kaiser averages for fiscal years ending June 1964 and June 1965.
[c] Includes capital stock, earned surplus, and surplus reserves.
*Source:* Annual company reports.

*(pesos per million pesos of output of the industry)*

| Input Industry | Direct Inputs | Import Co-efficient | Indirect Import Inputs (col. 1 × col. 2) |
|---|---|---|---|
| Fuel and electric | 8,367 | .168 | 1,411 |
| Textiles | 5,814 | .026 | 153 |
| Paper and cardboard | 4,431 | .068 | 306 |
| Printing and publishing | 887 | .143 | 128 |
| Chemical products | 24,655 | .125 | 3,104 |
| Rubber | 48,179 | .210 | 10,142 |
| Leather | 546 | .003 | 2 |
| Stone, glass, and ceramics | 1,793 | .045 | 81 |
| Metal working | 153,607 | .212 | 32,745 |
| Vehicles and machinery (including autos & tractors) | 25,488 | .160 | 4,098 |
| Machinery and electrical apparatus | 40,043 | .134 | 5,403 |
| Commerce | 106,610 | – | – |
| Transport | 21,320 | .001 | 25 |
| Services | 15,077 | .001 | 19 |
| Subtotal: national inputs | 456,817 | .126 | 57,617 |
| Imported inputs | 147,151 | 1.000 | 147,151 |
| Value added at market prices | 396,032 | 0.100[b] | 39,603 |
| Total | 1,000,000 | | 244,370 |

[a] Includes tractors.

[b] Estimate of foreign remittances for licensing fees, interest on debt, and profits (10 percent of ex-factory price).

*Source:* Consejo Nacional de Desarrollo (CONADE), *Matrix of Co-efficients of National and Imported Inputs*, 1960.

ANNEX TABLE 20: Yugoslav Exports of Vehicles and Parts, 1965

| | Total Import Value (US$ millions)[a] | Total Export Value (US$ millions)[a] | Export as Percent of Import |
|---|---|---|---|
| Ambulances | 0.1 | 0.4 | 461 |
| Trucks (1–3 tons) | 0.4 | 1.2 | 305 |
| Interurban and tourist buses | 0.3 | 0.8 | 245 |
| Crane vehicles | 0.6 | 0.7 | 117 |
| Cars up to 1110 Cm$^3$ | 4.3 | 4.2 | 98 |
| City traffic buses | 0.5 | 0.4 | 77 |
| Trucks (3–5 tons) | 1.6 | 1.1 | 69 |
| Motorcycle vehicles and parts | 1.5 | 1.0 | 63 |
| Truck and bus engines and engine parts | 4.8 | 3.0 | 62 |
| Motor vehicle parts[b] | 7.2 | 3.5 | 49 |
| Other special motor vehicles | 0.8 | 0.3 | 35 |
| Trucks in assembly parts | 3.8 | 1.1 | 29 |
| Heavy trucks (over 5 tons) | 7.2 | 1.4 | 20 |
| Car engines and engine parts | 1.4 | 0.1 | 9 |
| Cars, 1110 Cm$^3$–2500 Cm$^3$ | 9.5 | 0.7 | 8 |
| Chassis with engines and bodies[c] | 0.9 | 0.1 | 6 |
| Total | 44.9 | 20.0 | 45 |

[a] Converted from dinar values at 1965 dinar rate of 300 to the US dollar.

[b] Gear boxes, differential and other transmission parts, wheels and axles, road tractor assembly parts and other motor vehicle parts.

[c] Including buses, trucks, and other motor vehicles.

Source: B.P.M.V. (Automotive Constructors Bureau), The Yugoslav Industry, 1965.

| Company | Product | Units | Percentage Distribution |
|---|---|---|---|
| Ford Motor Company of New Zealand Ltd. | Anglia | 2,118 | 3.3 |
| | Cortina | 4,898 | 7.7 |
| | Zephyr/Zodiac | 3,103 | 4.9 |
| | Falcon | 2,128 | 3.3 |
| | Other | 90 | 0.2 |
| | Total | 12,337 | 19.4 |
| General Motors New Zealand Ltd. | Vauxhall | 6,470 | 10.2 |
| | Holden | 8,651 | 13.6 |
| | Chevrolet | 394 | 0.6 |
| | Pontiac | 201 | 0.3 |
| | Other | 36 | 0.1 |
| | Total | 15,752 | 24.8 |
| Todd Motors Ltd. | Hillman/Hunter | 5,742 | 9.0 |
| | Chrysler | 3,033 | 4.8 |
| | Singer | 573 | 0.9 |
| | Renault | 325 | 0.5 |
| | Other | 53 | 0.1 |
| | Total | 9,726 | 15.3 |
| The Dominion Motors Ltd. | Morris/Nuffield | 8,716 | 13.7 |
| | Wolseley | 905 | 1.4 |
| | Total | 9,621 | 15.1 |
| Austin Distributors Ltd. | Austin Mini | 1,648 | 2.6 |
| | Austin 1100 | 2,289 | 3.6 |
| | Austin 1800 | 1,667 | 2.6 |
| | Other | 228 | 0.4 |
| | Total | 5,832 | 9.2 |

| Company | Product | Units | Percentage Distribution |
|---|---|---|---|
| Motor Industries (International) Ltd. | Volkswagen | 2,491 | 3.9 |
| | Fiat | 1,318 | 2.1 |
| | Skoda | 416 | 0.6 |
| | Simca | 374 | 0.6 |
| | Total | 4,599 | 7.2 |
| Leyland Standard Triumph | Triumph | 2,331 | 3.7 |
| Steel Bros. (Addington) | Toyota | 23 | – |
| | Prince | 614 | 1.0 |
| | Total | 637 | 1.0 |
| Campbell Industries Ltd. | Peugeot | 380 | 0.6 |
| | Hino | 266 | 0.4 |
| | Rambler | 332 | 0.5 |
| | Isusu | 8 | – |
| | Datsun | 349 | 0.6 |
| | Total | 1,335 | 2.1 |
| Other companies | | 1,397 | 2.2 |
| Total (all companies) | 47 | 63,567 | 100.0 |

*Source:* Report by New Zealand vehicle manufacturer.

## ANNEX TABLE 22: Personal-Income/Car-Price Ratios in Selected Countries, 1966

| Country | New Passenger Car Registrations ('000) | Average Annual Income of Hourly Rate Employee in Auto Industry (US$) | Retail Purchase Price (including all taxes) of Highest Sales Volume Passenger Car | | |
|---|---|---|---|---|---|
| | | | Cars | Price (US$) | Percent of Income |
| Argentina | 129.7 | 2,173 | Fiat-1500 | 5,067 | 233 |
| Australia | 303.8 | 3,097 | Holden | 2,427 | 78 |
| Brazil | 157.2 | 1,838 | Volkswagen | 2,530 | 138 |
| France | 1,216.0 | 2,630 | Citroën-Ami 6 | 1,478 | 56 |
| Germany | 1,506.7 | 2,980 | Volkswagen | 1,288 | 43 |
| Italy | 1,014.9 | 2,542 | Fiat-500D | 766 | 30 |
| Japan | 740.9 | 2,189 | Toyota Corona | 1,567 | 72 |
| Mexico | 83.4 | 3,025 | Volkswagen | 1,904 | 63 |
| Sweden | 208.0 | 4,842 | Volvo | 3,105 | 64 |
| United Kingdom | 1,053.2 | 3,240 | Ford-Cortina | 1,845 | 57 |
| United States | 8,980.0 | 8,218 | Chevrolet Impala | 3,054 | 37 |
| Venezuela | 19.5 | 3,995 | Volkswagen | 2,362 | 59 |

*Source:* Table furnished by US manufacturer.